Contents

INTRODUCTION

SECTION 1 Reading *Student book Units 1, 2 and 5*
  Short-answer comprehension questions   4
  Writer's effects questions   14
  Practice exercises   19

SECTION 2 Directed writing *Student book Units 7 and 10*
  Extended response to reading exercises   34
  Directed writing exercises   55

SECTION 3 Writing summaries *Student book Units 3, 6 and 8*
  Writing a summary   60
  Summary writing exercises   61

SECTION 4 Writing compositions *Student book Units 4, 9, 11 and 12*
  Structure   80
  Vocabulary   83
  Accuracy of expression   84
  Composition writing exercises   85

Introduction

Welcome to the *Cambridge IGCSE™ First Language English Workbook*. This book is designed to complement the fifth edition of the student book and to provide additional exercises to help you develop and practise the skills and concepts you are learning during your course.

Links to the relevant units in the student book can be found in the contents list as well as at the start of each section. Each section contains a range of practice exercises with questions that follow the style of those from Papers 1 and 2 of the Cambridge IGCSE First Language English examination. These will help you develop your skills and practise applying them to a range of questions, and also help you in your preparation for examination by becoming familiar with the types of questions. Support for coursework and the speaking and listening test can be found in the student book.

Answers are available FREE to download from: hachettelearning.com/answers-and-extras

1 Reading

Student book, Units 1, 2 and 5

Short-answer comprehension questions

The exercises that follow will help you develop your skills in active reading, comprehension and understanding of writer's effects. Remember to concentrate on the following points:

- Read both the passage and the questions carefully before you start to answer the questions.
- Underline or highlight the key words in each question.
- When answering the questions, use your own words whenever possible in order to show your understanding of what you have read.
- The marks shown at the end of each question can be an indication of how many points you should make in your answer. For example, if there are 2 marks available for the question, then you should give two distinct points in your answer.

Exercise 1

Read carefully the following extract from an article about the North-west Passage by Sarah Barrell. Then answer the questions that follow, using your own words as far as possible.

By way of background, it is useful to know that the North-west Passage is a sea route through the Arctic Ocean via the islands of northern Canada, connecting the Atlantic and Pacific oceans. Explorers spent centuries trying to locate it in order to provide a much quicker shipping route between Europe and Asia. Although such a route exists, navigating it is challenging and it is only accessible between July and September as this is the only time of the year that the ice has reduced sufficiently to allow ships through.

The North-west Passage: A 21st-century expedition

By Sarah Barrell

A cruise, led by Inuit people, follows the early explorers around the Canadian Arctic in waters that are still largely uncharted. Sarah Barrell went aboard.

Summer in the Arctic and dust, not snow, covers the ground. In Gjoa Haven, an Inuit settlement on King William, an island in the heart of the North-west Passage, there's dust on the seats of skidoos. Dust, too, on the coats of the scrappy sled dogs that are tethered in long lines waiting for winter and starter's orders.

About them, teenagers charge around on battered all-terrain vehicles, kicking up more dust, making the most of the light evenings and the comparatively balmy 10 °C temperatures. It's hard to imagine amid all this, with the sun shooting in laser-bright arcs off the town's tin-roofed houses, that somewhere in or around this island, Sir John Franklin, an intrepid 19th-century Arctic explorer, met a dark and icy end trying to discover the fabled North-west Passage.

He vanished more than a century and a half ago, but the fever to find the remains of Franklin's expedition still runs high in the remote Canadian Arctic, some 5000 kilometres from the shores of the UK. Earlier this summer, Canadian authorities unveiled the wreck of HMS *Investigator*, one

Short-answer comprehension questions

→ of the many doomed 19th-century rescue ships sent in search of Franklin's expedition. Then, just last week in the town of Gjoa Haven itself, archaeologists unearthed what could be the Holy Grail of Arctic exploration history. At the behest of local brothers Wally and Andrew Porter, a box was excavated containing, the Porters claim, long sought-after records from the ill-fated Franklin expedition that might reveal its final whereabouts.

Franklin was more advanced in age and overweight than other explorers of his era; his ships were also spectacularly over-burdened when he left for his third Arctic expedition in 1845. The British Admiralty brushed this aside as the fervour to conquer the North-west Passage once again reached a peak. There was prize money at stake (£20,000 [USD 28,000] offered by the British crown) for anyone who could navigate the elusive, icy waterway connecting the Atlantic and Pacific oceans. But beyond this, there was the chance to forge crucial northern trade links between Europe and Asia, one that would open up a new route to the spice lands and, in addition, avoid stormy sailings around Cape Horn. But was Franklin the man to fly Britain's flag into the uncharted north?

Probably not, given that he had survived his first expedition charting Canada's Arctic coast by eating his own boots and being rescued by Native Americans. There was much that European explorers could learn from the three centuries of sailors who had battled to find a northerly route connecting the Atlantic and Pacific – in short, to travel light and use local expertise. Instead, highlighting the egotism of the time, Franklin's expedition sailed out of London laden with chests of fine china, dead-weight sledges and canned food that would later finish them off with lead-poisoning. After three winters trapped in ice, Franklin's crew abandoned their two ships, the *Erebus* and *Terror*, somewhere off the coast of King William Island and were never seen again.

I manage to stop at this remote part of the Arctic Archipelago on board an eight-day tour, uniquely led by a local Inuit team. In true expedition style, there are no promised ports of call as conditions can change suddenly. Our first two days' passage is devoid of ice or high seas, but we hear that another cruise ship has run aground in shallow straits to the far west. 'Even with the ice receding, there's only been clear passage here for about five years,' says Dugald Wells, President of Cruise North, a former marine engineer who has been working in the Arctic since the mid-1980s. 'I came up here because it was fun – a real frontier. It still is, but you have to respect the fact that only 50 per cent of these waters are surveyed,' he says.

Adapted from *The Independent*, 19 September 2010

1 What is the most noticeable feature of summer in the Arctic mentioned in paragraph 1 (after the introductory bold text)? [1]

....

2 Give two possible reasons as to why the writer describes the sled dogs as 'scrappy'. [2]

- ....

  ....

- ....

  ....

1 READING

3 a Which word in paragraph 3 tells you that the box found by archaeologists had been buried in the ground? [1]

....

b What information did the Porter brothers hope that it would contain? [1]

....

4 By referring to paragraph 4, explain why Sir John Franklin's ships were unsuited to the Arctic voyage. [1]

5 From paragraph 4, give two reasons why the British Admiralty placed so much importance on discovering the North-west Passage. [2]

- ....

....

- ....

....

6 By referring to paragraph 5, explain fully, using your own words:

a the writer's criticisms of Franklin's expedition [1]

....

....

....

....

b the outcome of the expedition. [1]

....

....

7 Explain, using your own words, why the writer says in the final paragraph that on the Arctic tour, 'there are no promised ports of call'. [1]

....

....

Exercise 2

In the following blog post, Aditi Chawla gives an account of a memorable encounter while researching the animal population of the Great Himalayan National Park. Read the extract and then answer the questions that follow.

An unexpected encounter

By Aditi Chawla

It was spring when we visited the Great Himalayan National Park in Himachal Pradesh, a UNESCO World Heritage Site in the far Western Himalayas. It had been a cold, snowy winter and feeling the gentle warmth in the air, seeing the blossoms, filled us with excitement and optimism about the trip ahead. We paused before the entrance to extend our greetings to GB's Hippo. Sadly, the hippo is really no more than a large sedentary bolder but, sat as he was at the bottom of a small waterfall, it was easy to convince ourselves that he had just dunked his head under the water momentarily and would soon raise it to look at us. As we set off, the sound of the Tirthan River echoed around us, its waters swollen with the receding snow of early spring. Only as we ventured deeper into the forest was it drowned out by the howling of the wind. The beauty of the place distracted me, and I lagged behind my companions and our guide, Kabir, only catching up when we arrived at a diversion point.

We were visiting the park as part of our research and had been given permission by the National Mission on Himalayan Studies (NMHS) and the Wildlife Institute of India to enter some parts not normally accessible to visitors. Crossing an old wooden bridge, we found ourselves at the beginning of a natural path which seemed to have been formed by the movement of animals heading down to a point on the river which was easy to cross. It was here that we set our first camera trap, a movement-sensitive device which allowed us to capture images of the wildlife with little human interference. With this work done, we headed uphill, aware of the weight of our packs on our backs, as we reminded ourselves that it was the park's wide range of elevation which was in part responsible for its beautiful and diverse plant life.

The ascent took us into thick oak forest. Sometimes we could hear the Tirthan but at other times the sound seemed unable to penetrate the thick vegetation around us. For some of the way we had chatted in quiet voices, talking about our work or pointing out interesting vegetation, but soon the trek became too difficult and we fell silent. Perhaps taking this as his cue, Kabir suggested that we catch our breaths and have the meals that we had packed, and we looked around us, waiting for him to advise whether it was a good place to stop. All around were patches of freshly dug-up earth. 'Bhalu,' Kabir said, the Hindi word for bear. It was evidence of bears searching for insects and mites, he said, adding that this part of the forest was a good place for sighting the endangered Himalayan Brown Bear.

And then, as if his voice had called it into existence, there before us was an adult Himalayan Brown Bear, at work on the ground, using its long claws to dig through the earth. We all froze, with the animal no less than 20m away. We'd stopped to catch our breath but now we stood holding our breaths as the animal sensed our presence and stood to face us. Its nostrils flared and it seemed to look me directly in the eye. Had the bear been with a cub, it might have charged us and our story would have had a different ending, but instead it turned and sprinted off, surprisingly agile given its large size. We watched its beautiful golden-brown body disappear into the trees.

For a moment we remained frozen until Kabir, pointing to the equipment that we carried on our backs, said, 'So many cameras, no picture.' We all laughed although it was only then, after the moment of absolute fear was gone that I wondered why I hadn't grabbed at the phone that was hanging on a strap around my neck, and taken a picture. I have on occasion taken a picture to →

1 READING

share, of a delicious meal I've been served at a restaurant or something funny that I've seen in a shop. But the day I came face to face with the endangered Himalayan Brown Bear I didn't think to take a picture!

Once we'd all recovered from our fright, we felt an unexpected sense of elation. There are between 500 and 750 Himalayan Brown Bears left in India and we'd just seen one of them close up. It's not often that you experience something that you know will probably never happen to you again in your life; or something that you know you are one of a very few people to have experienced. We set up a camera trap nearby, so perhaps we will have a picture of our friend in time, but energised by the experience we decided to press on.

Walking through the forest we emerged into a lush meadow full of spring blossoms. From there, across a brook, our campsite came into view. In the hut, Kabir lit a fire and made us cups of tea. Perhaps it was only then that we were able to truly relax, letting go of the suppressed hysteria that had powered us through the walk to the camp. As the sun began to set, we sat on the ground outside of the hut and looked at the warm glow of the butter-coloured sky. I might have felt grateful to be alive and uninjured (and believe me, I was!) but in the twilight I was even more aware of the beauty of the place and most of all felt gratitude for the encounter itself. It's a rare thing to be so close to such a beautiful animal in its natural habitat, and it may be impossible to describe the magic of connecting with a species so different from our own. But it's a reminder of why we must work so hard to protect endangered animals and to preserve habitat, not just for their sake but for our own.

1 From paragraph 1 what two details tell us that winter was ending in the Himalayas? [2]

2 What is meant by the word 'sedentary' and how does it help you to visualise the rock in the waterfall (paragraph 1)? [2]

3 What sounds could the writer hear as they 'ventured deeper into the forest' (paragraph 1)? [2]

4 Explain as fully as you can what the writer and her colleagues were doing in the National Park and their reason for being there. [3]

Short-answer comprehension questions

5 Give details of where they were in the forest when they encountered the bear and what alerted Kabir to its presence. *[3]*

....

....

....

6 In your own words, describe the bear's response to seeing the humans and explain why it behaved as it did. *[2]*

....

....

....

7 Explain, using your own words, why the writer was surprised that she didn't think to take a photograph of the bear. *[2]*

....

....

8 By referring to the final paragraph, explain as fully as you can, the writer's reflections on her encounter with the bear. *[4]*

....

....

....

....

....

1 READING

Exercise 3
Read the following article carefully and then answer the questions that follow.

Experience: I was swept away by a flood

By Vanessa Glover

'Shocked, tossed and buffeted, I gasped for breath and tried to keep my head above water.'

It was after midnight last December and we were driving home from a party. There had been extremely heavy rain on our journey there, though not enough to make us worry about the drive back. We were in our pick-up truck, which always felt safe. Paul, my husband, was driving and my seven-year-old son, Silas, was in the back.

What was so frightening was the speed of it. One minute we were halfway home and driving up to a familiar bridge, the next there was water rising over the bonnet. Deep floodwater was coursing across from a nearby railway line and surrounding fields, and we were caught in the middle of it.

The volume of water lifted our car up and pushed it back against a hedge. We were silent; I felt over-awed by the power of the water, and Paul was trying to control the truck.

Water was instantly around my ankles. I reached my hand back and felt it around Silas's, too. Paul climbed out through a window, at which point Silas woke up, confused and disoriented. I managed to pass him through the window to Paul, who was now on the truck's roof.

Paul told me I needed to get out, but I couldn't open my door or window. I managed to push my body though the driver's window and was left clinging onto the support between the windows. I was terrified the truck would capsize, pinning me beneath. Paul was incredulous, asking me what I was doing in the water, and telling me I needed to climb onto the bonnet, but I couldn't reach.

He grabbed my hood to help, but I could hear Silas crying, so I told him to let go – Silas needed him. He refused, but I insisted – I wanted to know Silas would be OK. As I saw his empty, outstretched hand, the water took me away. I'm a strong swimmer, but had no option but to shoot down the rapids. Shocked, tossed and buffeted, I gasped for breath and tried to keep my head above water. There was a horrendously loud noise, like a huge wall of bubbles swirling in my ears. I never expected to die of drowning.

I was washed over a garden wall into the river, 3.5 m higher than normal and flowing at about 23 kph. It was extremely dark but I could just make out trees. I reached out and grabbed two branches no bigger than my index finger, with a perfect tight grip. Somehow my feet wedged in a firm foothold and I hugged the tree with my knees. Another minute, and I'd have been sucked beneath a railway bridge.

My plan was just to hold on. My body went into shock a few times and I trembled involuntarily. I told myself it was a natural response and concentrated on not losing my foothold. Not knowing if Paul and Silas were dead or alive, I thought that if they survived they would need me.

After nearly 40 minutes, I saw a small spotlight. I shouted for help. Someone glimpsed my movement and a firefighter tried to talk to me, but I couldn't hear her above the roar of the water.

The light of a helicopter made me out in the tree. Their heat-seeking equipment had traced me, but they could see I had no warmth in my lower body and were concerned I would become hypothermic and lose my grip. My husband, who had been rescued with my son in the bucket of a mechanical digger, was nearby with a policewoman. She reassured him that so long as they could hear me, there was hope.

Short-answer comprehension questions

> → Guided to me by the helicopter, the rescue team managed to steer the boat to my shoulder. Four strong arms lifted me into the boat and I felt sheer relief and utter safety.
>
> My rescuers were volunteers who have since received medals and I have an incredibly deep bond with them. In the isolation of that tree, I found a strength of character I didn't know I possessed – but I'm still flabbergasted I survived at all.
>
> Adapted from *The Guardian*, 15 June 2013

1 Why had the writer and her family been out late at night (paragraph 1, after the introductory bold text)? [1]

  ....

2 By referring closely to paragraphs 2 and 3, explain carefully what you learn about the flood and how it affected the car in which the writer was travelling. [3]

  ....

  ....

  ....

3 Using your own words, explain carefully Silas's state of mind when he woke up (paragraph 4). [2]

  ....

  ....

4 Why was the writer afraid of the truck capsizing (paragraph 5)? [1]

  ....

5 What two things was the writer concerned about while she was hugging the tree (paragraph 8)? [2]

  • ....

  • ....

6 How can you tell how many people hauled the writer into the rescue boat (paragraph 11)? [1]

  ....

7 Which word in the final paragraph tells you that the writer was completely amazed by the outcome of her experience? [1]

  ....

Photocopying prohibited

1 READING

Exercise 4

The following passage is an extract from the short story 'The Country of the Blind' by H.G. Wells. Nunez, an explorer in the Andes mountain range in South America, has fallen down a mountainside onto a rocky ledge where he has spent the night. Read the passage carefully and then answer the questions that follow.

He was awakened by the singing of birds in the trees far below. He sat up and perceived he was at the foot of a vast precipice. Over against him another wall of rock reared itself against the sky. The gorge between these precipices ran east and west. It was full of the morning sunlight, which lit the mass of fallen mountain to the west. Below him it seemed there was a precipice equally steep, but behind the snow in the gully he found a sort of chimney-cleft dripping with snow-water, down which a desperate man might venture. He found it easier than it seemed and after a rock climb of no particular difficulty came to a steep slope of trees.

He turned his face up the gorge and saw it opened out above onto green meadows, among which he glimpsed a cluster of stone huts of unfamiliar fashion. At times his progress was like clambering along the face of a wall, and after a time the rising sun ceased to strike along the gorge, the voices of the singing birds died away, and the air grew cold and dark about him. But the distant valley with its houses was all the brighter for that. Among the rocks he noted an unfamiliar fern. He picked a frond or so and gnawed its stalk, and found it helpful.

About midday he came at last out of the gorge into the plain and the sunlight. He was stiff and weary; he sat down in the shadow of a rock, filled up his flask with water from a spring and drank it down. He remained for a time, resting before he went on to the houses.

They were very strange to his eyes, and indeed the whole appearance of that valley became, as he regarded it, stranger and more unfamiliar. The greater part of its surface was lush green meadow, starred with many beautiful flowers. It was irrigated with extraordinary care, and showed signs of systematic farming. High up and ringing the valley about was a wall, and what appeared to be a water channel, from which the little trickles of water that fed the meadow plants came. On the higher slopes flocks of llamas cropped the scanty grass. The irrigation streams ran together into a main channel down the centre of the valley, and this was enclosed on either side by a wall chest high. A number of paths paved with black and white stones, and each with a curious little kerb at the side, ran here and there in an orderly manner.

The houses of the central village were quite unlike those of the mountain villages he knew. They stood in a continuous row on either side of a central street of astonishing cleanness. Here and there their walls were pierced by a door, but not a solitary window broke their even frontage. They were parti-coloured with extraordinary irregularity, smeared with a sort of plaster that was sometimes grey, sometimes drab, sometimes slate-coloured or dark brown. It was the sight of this wild plastering that made the explorer say to himself, 'The good man who did that must have been as blind as a bat.'

He descended a steep place, and so came to the wall and channel that ran about the valley. He could now see a number of men and women resting on piled heaps of grass, as if taking a siesta, in the remoter part of the meadow. Nearer the village a number of children were lying on their backs, and then coming closer to him he saw three men. These men wore garments of llama cloth and boots and belts of leather, and caps of cloth with back and ear flaps. They followed one another in single file, walking slowly and yawning as they walked, like men who have been up all night. There was something so reassuringly prosperous and respectable in their bearing that after a moment's hesitation Nunez stood forward as conspicuously as possible upon his rock, and gave vent to a mighty shout that echoed round the valley.

From 'The Country of the Blind' by H.G. Wells

Short-answer comprehension questions

1 What caused Nunez to wake up? [1]

   ....

2 Using your own words, explain carefully how Nunez reached the slope of trees from the precipice on which he awoke. [2]

   ....

   ....

   ....

3 By referring closely to the second half of paragraph 2 ('But the distant ... and found it helpful.'), state three things that the writer says that Nunez saw. [3]

   • ....

   • ....

   • ....

4 Why did the air grow 'cold and dark' (paragraph 2)? [1]

   ....

   ....

5 Explain, using your own words, the sentence: 'It was irrigated with extraordinary care, and showed signs of systematic farming.' (paragraph 4). [2]

   ....

   ....

   ....

6 State two unusual things about the appearance of the village (paragraph 5). [2]

   • ....

   ....

   • ....

   ....

Photocopying prohibited   Cambridge IGCSE™ First Language English Workbook 3rd Edition

1 READING

Writer's effects questions

As well as showing an understanding of the vocabulary used by writers, another key skill that you need to develop is to understand (or appreciate) the way that writers use language to produce a particular response from their readers. The following group of questions allows you to practise both explaining the meaning of some key words in the passages on which they are based and also test your appreciation of how the writer's use of language creates a particular effect in the mind of the reader.

It is important to keep in mind that questions 1c and 1d in the following exercises ask you to explain how the language used by writers achieves particular effects. They do not ask you simply to explain the meanings of the words used. (Although it goes without saying that the best responses are likely to come from students who have a clear understanding of the meanings.)

In this section of the workbook, you will have the opportunity to practise writing answers to these types of questions in response to a range of passages.

The instructions for question 1d state that in order to answer the question, you should select 'powerful words and phrases' from the stimulus passage. It is also stated that the words or phrases chosen should contain **imagery**.

What is meant by imagery (and how to write about it)

Imagery means the use of figurative language (such as simile, metaphor, onomatopoeia, alliteration, personification, and so on) to represent objects, actions and ideas in such a way that there is an appeal to our physical senses. Imagery works initially by producing a picture in the mind of a reader. However, the range of associations with the vocabulary used by a writer to create the image is likely to produce secondary responses in the reader by appealing to other senses in addition to sight.

The basic tool that all writers use to communicate with their readers is their vocabulary – the words that they choose. For readers to understand what a writer is saying to them, it is important that they interpret the words as having the same meaning that the writers had in their minds when they chose them. This is particularly important in writing that is intended to give information or instruction. For example, if the reader of a medical textbook misunderstands the word *diseased* and assumes that the writer has written *deceased*, there may be considerable problems in store for future patients!

It is, of course, highly important that the vocabulary used in instructional writing should convey a clear and unambiguous meaning. However, in imaginative or personal writing, writers use language not to give instructions but in order to appeal to their readers' emotions and imaginations and to create a multi-dimensional response. One way by which this effect is achieved is when the reader responds not just to the meanings of the words in their immediate context, but to other associations that are carried by those words.

To take a straightforward example – if you hear someone shout the word *duck*, what does that mean to you? If you are an ornithologist (a person who studies birds), your first thought will be of a feathered flying creature. If you are in the park, you might respond by lowering your head or throwing yourself on the ground to avoid a flying ball. If you are a cricketer, you are likely to assume that the batsman has not been very successful. Or, if your mind is not focused on anything in particular, you might respond by associating any or all of these meanings together!

Such a reaction as that mentioned above is not highly likely when the different meanings of a word (such as *duck*) are clearly distinct. However, in much imaginative writing, the associations of the words used by a writer are much more closely linked. Readers who are fully engaged in the text will respond to what the writer has written by adding their own responses to the vocabulary and thereby creating a more complex response to what they are reading. This is sometimes referred to as responding to meanings *beyond the literal*.

Writer's effects questions

Some linguistic devices

The intention of the previous paragraphs was to help you to understand what you should do when you are asked to comment on a writer's use of language in the phrases you have chosen. Although it is important to show a clear understanding of the writer's overall intention, you must also do your best to show how your interpretation of the vocabulary, and the imagery that it creates, helps to develop and communicate the full implications of the writer's intention.

Writers create imagery through the use of linguistic devices. There is not space here to provide an exhaustive list of the different linguistic devices that can be found, nor is it appropriate to do so. However, below is a brief list of the main linguistic devices that are likely to occur in the passages that you will read, together with definitions and examples of their use.

> **Key point**
>
> When commenting on a writer's use of language, it is important to keep in mind that you should comment on how writers achieve their effects and not what linguistic devices they use in order to do so. It is not enough simply to identify similes, metaphors, etc. in a piece of writing – it is necessary to explain what the effects of their use are on a reader.

Simile

A simile is a direct comparison between two things, introduced by the word *like* or *as*, in order to make a description more vivid or emphatic. For example, in John Steinbeck's novel *Of Mice and Men*, the following phrase is used to describe the relationship between the character Lennie (who has learning disabilities) and his friend and protector George.

Lennie is like a terrier who doesn't want to bring its ball to its master.

The comparison between Lennie and a dog helps to convey to the reader that Lennie's intelligence is little more than that of an animal. It also presents a more sympathetic picture of him by showing that he is both dependent on his friend as well as being a little afraid that he may have done something to upset him for which he may be scolded.

Metaphor

A metaphor is an indirect comparison in which one thing is expressed in terms of another – there is no need to use *like* or *as*. For example, a character in one of Shakespeare's plays says that:

All the world's a stage and all the men and women merely players.

He is not suggesting that literally everyone in the world lives and performs inside a theatre, but is using the comparison between the world and a stage in a symbolic way to suggest that we all behave ('act') in different ways in different circumstances.

Onomatopoeia

Onomatopoeia is a term used to describe the effect created by a writer when the sound of a word or words echoes the sense of what is being described, and helps to bring the description alive in the mind of the reader. In its simplest form, words like 'bang' and 'crash' are examples of onomatopoeia. A more complex example is the following description from W.B. Yeats's poem 'The Lake Isle of Innisfree':

Nine bean-rows will I have there, a hive for the honey-bee;

And live alone in the bee-loud glade.

The description of the peace of the island is enhanced for the reader as the long, open vowel sounds of 'bee-loud glade' convey the buzzing sound of the bees which is emphasised by the surrounding quiet.

Alliteration

Alliteration is the term given to the repetition of the same sound(s) at the beginning of words. At its simplest level, this is the main device used in tongue-twisters such as 'Peter Piper picked a peck of

Photocopying prohibited

1 READING

pickled pepper'. However, in D.H. Lawrence's poem 'Snake', the repetition of the 's' sound at the start of the words in the following lines very effectively suggests the hissing sound of a snake:

He sipped with his straight mouth,

Softly drank through his straight gums, into his slack long body,

Silently.

Personification

Personification is the term given to the literary technique of attributing human characteristics to inanimate objects or non-human life forms, as in the following famous lines from William Wordsworth's description of a wood full of daffodils:

Ten thousand saw I at a glance,

Tossing their heads in sprightly dance.

> **Key point**
>
> The use of one linguistic device can easily blend in with that of another. In the example of alliteration from the poem 'Snake', the lines also have an onomatopoeic effect, and the example of personification is also a type of metaphor. As mentioned earlier, you should not worry too much about identifying examples of linguistic devices – what is important is that you recognise their effect on a reader and then explain how this effect is achieved.

The description of the flowers, which suggests that they were like exuberant and carefree human dancers, gives a vivid impression of the scene and also helps the readers to identify with the poet's response to the flowers.

Although the use of literary devices such as those mentioned above is the main way in which writers create imagery, you might also need to consider how things such as sentence structure and the length of sentences contribute to the overall effect that a writer achieves.

Types of questions

The different types of questions in the following exercises test both your understanding of the vocabulary used in the accompanying passages and of how the writer of the passage has used language to create particular responses in a reader's mind.

- Question 1a requires you to write down words or phrases from the text with the same meaning as those underlined in four sentences given in the question. Note that when answering this question it is important that you write down only the word or group of words that relate directly to those that you are defining.

- Question 1b requires you to explain in your own words the meanings of three words used in the passage. Note that it is important when answering this question that you explain only the words underlined in the question, that you explain the word in the context of the passage in which it occurs and that you do not use the same word as a different part of speech in your answer. For example, it would be wrong to define the word 'scream' in the following sentence 'The child gave a scream of excitement on opening his present' by saying 'screamed excitedly'. If you cannot think of a single word to replace that underlined in the question, you can use a short phrase to define it.

- Question 1c requires you to explain in your own words how specific words or phrases used by the writer in a short section of the passage suggest a particular atmosphere, experience or feeling. Note that when responding to this question it is important that you give evidence that you have some appreciation of the associations and suggestions in the writer's choice of words.

- Question 1d refers you to two sections of the passage and then requires you to select four words or phrases from each section (that is, eight words or phrases in total) that produce a particular effect or response in the mind of the reader. You should explain how each of your selections is used effectively in the context of the passage. Note that in answering this question, it is important that you show understanding and appreciation of the imagery used by the writer and that you focus on explaining how the language creates a particular effect and not on simply identifying and naming any linguistic devices that you recognise.

Example of a writer's effects questions

The following passage is a satirical description of a lesson in a school in 19th-century England, taken from the opening of Charles Dickens's *Hard Times*. Answer the questions that follow.

> 'Now, what I want is, Facts. Teach these boys and girls nothing but Facts. Facts alone are wanted in life. Plant nothing else, and root out everything else. You can only form the minds of reasoning animals upon Facts: nothing else will ever be of any service to them. This is the principle on which I bring up my own children, and this is the principle on which I bring up these children. Stick to Facts, sir!'
>
> The scene was a plain, bare, monotonous vault of a school-room, and the speaker's square forefinger emphasised his observations by underscoring every sentence with a line on the schoolmaster's sleeve. The emphasis was helped by the speaker's square wall of a forehead, which had his eyebrows for its base, while his eyes found commodious cellarage in two dark caves, overshadowed by the wall. The emphasis was helped by the speaker's mouth, which was wide, thin, and hard set. The emphasis was helped by the speaker's voice, which was inflexible, dry, and dictatorial. The emphasis was helped by the speaker's hair, which bristled on the skirts of his bald head, a plantation of firs to keep the wind from its shining surface, all covered with knobs, like the crust of a plum pie, as if the head had scarcely warehouse-room for the hard facts stored inside. The speaker's obstinate carriage, square coat, square legs, square shoulders,—nay, his very neckcloth, trained to take him by the throat with an unaccommodating grasp, like a stubborn fact, as it was,—all helped the emphasis.
>
> 'In this life, we want nothing but Facts, sir; nothing but Facts!'
>
> The speaker, and the schoolmaster, and the third grown person present, all backed a little, and swept with their eyes the inclined plane of little vessels then and there arranged in order, ready to have imperial gallons of facts poured into them until they were full to the brim.
>
> From *Hard Times* by Charles Dickens

1 a Identify a word or phrase from the text that conveys the same idea as the words underlined:

   i He thought that facts were essential for shaping the minds of <u>rational beings</u>.

   (Answer: reasoning animals)

   ii It is on this <u>premise</u> that I have based the education of my children.

   (Answer: principle)

   iii The underground cavern provided <u>large storage space</u> for his equipment.

   (Answer: commodious cellarage)

   iv He spoke to us in such a <u>domineering</u> way that we had to do what he said.

   (Answer: dictatorial)

1 READING

b Explain, in your own words, what the writer means by each of the words underlined:

'The speaker's <u>obstinate</u> carriage, square coat, square legs, square shoulders,—nay, his very neckcloth, trained to take him by the throat with an <u>unaccommodating</u> grasp, like a stubborn fact, as it was,—all helped the <u>emphasis</u>.'

(Answer: obstinate – inflexible / refusal to change his mind)

(Answer: unaccommodating – uncooperative / intractable / not accepting other suggestions)

(Answer: emphasis – forcefulness / weight / stress)

c Explain, in your own words, how the underlined phrases are used by the writer to suggest the character of the speaker:

'The speaker's <u>obstinate carriage</u>, square coat, square legs, square shoulders,—nay, his very neckcloth, trained to <u>take him by the throat with an unaccommodating grasp</u>, like a stubborn fact, as it was,—<u>all helped the emphasis</u>.'

(Answer: The words 'obstinate carriage' suggest that the speaker is like a heavy and inflexible vehicle that once moving cannot be stopped. 'Take him by the throat with an unaccommodating grasp' further suggests that the speaker is rough and violent in defence of his beliefs and will use force to ensure that others agree with him. 'All helped the emphasis' implies that the speaker will use all of his strength and threatening nature to force home his ideas on other people in the room.)

d Re-read the second paragraph of the passage and then identify four powerful words or groups of words that suggest the appearance of the school-room and the appearance and attitude of the man speaking. Your choices should include imagery. **Explain** how each of your chosen words or groups of words is used in the context of the passage.

(Answer: See below)

Student response

1 'a plain, bare, monotonous vault of a school-room'

The vocabulary in this phrase is direct and unadorned, reflecting the plain, uninteresting nature of the room. The list of three adjectives ('plain, bare, monotonous') builds up to emphasise effectively the stultifying surroundings in which the lesson is taking place. The noun 'vault' carries associations not just of a vast, empty space, but also hints that the room is like a cold burial chamber, reinforcing the idea that the school-room is part of the means by which the life of imagination is denied, as conveyed by the final line of the passage.

2 'the speaker's square wall of a forehead, which had his eyebrows for its base'

As befits someone who is in favour of only 'facts' being taught, the forehead of the speaker is described as 'square', which suggests that there is no scope for deviation from straight lines in his way of thinking. 'Wall' suggests solidity and the main purpose of a wall is to keep out trespassers; in this case, imaginative ideas. The image of the man as a mathematical creation is reinforced by the description of his eyebrows as being the base of the wall – 'base' is a word associated with triangles as well as walls.

3 'the speaker's hair, which bristled on the skirts of his bald head, a plantation of firs to keep the wind from its shining surface'

This is a mainly comic image which encourages the reader to see the man as someone deserving to be laughed at. (The writer is, after all, satirising his attitude and ideas.) The description of his hair as 'bristling' suggests that there is something about him that is looking to take offence. The metaphorical phrase ('a plantation of firs') again reinforces the point that his purpose is to prevent any unwanted thoughts (as suggested by the wind) from entering his mind.

4 'as if the head had scarcely warehouse-room for the hard facts stored inside'

Following on from the image of the 'vault' earlier in the passage, the word 'warehouse-room' conveys the idea of the speaker's mind, like the classroom, being a place in which commodities are stored. The commodities in this case are 'hard facts' – again, there is no need for any imagination in the speaker's outlook. The description of the facts as 'hard' suggests that they are harsh and unfriendly.

Practice exercises

Now is your opportunity to put into practice what you have learned about commenting on the way writers use language. The following six passages are all examples of descriptive writing, but are in a range of styles and written for a variety of purposes. They are all followed by exercises that provide a focus for your comments and are all suitable practice for Question 2 on Paper 1 (summary task). Some phrases have been highlighted in each passage to give an indication of suitable descriptions to comment on. However, as these exercises are intended to provide you with practice for answering this type of question in an examination, you should feel free to choose other phrases from the passages if you wish.

Exercise 5

The following passage is taken from the comic novel *The Third Policeman* by the Irish writer Flann O'Brien. In this extract, the narrator breaks into what he thinks is an empty house to look for a metal box hidden beneath the floorboards. Answer the questions that follow.

> I opened the iron gate and walked as softly as I could up the weed-tufted gravel drive. My mind was strangely empty. I felt no glow of pleasure and was unexcited at the prospect of becoming rich. I was occupied only with the mechanical task of finding a black box.
>
> The front-door was closed and set far back in a very deep porch. The wind and rain had whipped a coating of gritty dust against the panels and deep into the crack where the door opened, showing that it had been shut for years. Standing on a derelict flower-bed, I tried to push open the first window on the left. It yielded to my strength, raspingly and stubbornly. I clambered through the opening and found myself, not at once in a room, but crawling along the deepest window-ledge I had ever seen. After I had jumped noisily down upon the floor, I looked up and the open window seemed very far away and much too small to have admitted me.
>
> The room where I found myself was thick with dust, musty and empty of all furniture. Spiders had erected great stretchings of their web about the fireplace. I made my way quickly to the hall, threw open the door of the room where the box was and paused on the threshold. It was a dark morning and the weather had stained the windows with blears of grey wash which kept the brightest part of the weak light from coming in. The far corner of the room was a blur of shadow. I had a sudden urge to have done with my task and be out of this house forever. I walked across the bare boards, knelt down in the corner and passed my hands about the floor in search of the loose board. To my surprise I found it easily. It was about two feet in length and rocked hollowly under my hand. I lifted it up, laid it aside and struck a match. I saw a black metal cash-box nestling dimly in the hole. I put my hand down and crooked a finger into the loose reclining handle but the →

1 READING

> match suddenly flickered and went out and the handle of the box, which I had lifted up about an inch, slid heavily off my finger. Without stopping to light another match, I thrust my hand into the opening and, just when it should be closing about the box, something happened.
>
> I cannot hope to describe what it was but it had frightened me very much. It was some change which came upon me or upon the room, indescribably subtle, yet momentous. It was as if the daylight had changed with unnatural suddenness, as if the temperature had altered greatly in an instant or as if the air had become twice as rare or twice as dense as it had been in the twinkling of an eye. Perhaps all of these, or other things, happened together, for all my senses were bewildered all at once and could give me no explanation. The fingers of my right hand, thrust in the opening in the floor, had closed mechanically, found nothing at all, and came up again empty. The box had gone!
>
> I heard a cough behind me, soft and natural, yet more disturbing than any sound that could ever come upon the human ear. That I did not die of fright was due, I think, to two things: the fact that my senses were already disarranged and able to interpret to me only gradually what they had perceived and also the fact that the utterance of the cough seemed to bring with it some more awful alteration in everything. It was as if the universe stood still for an instant, suspending the planets in their courses. I collapsed weakly from my kneeling, backwards into a limp sitting-down position upon the floor. Sweat broke out on my brow and my eyes remained open for a long time without a wink, glazed and almost sightless.
>
> In the darkest corner of the room, near the window, a man was sitting in a chair, eyeing me with a mild but unwavering interest.
>
> From *The Third Policeman* by Flann O'Brien

1 a Identify a word or phrase from the text which conveys the same idea as the underlined words:

   i He thought the <u>possibility of finding a fortune</u> was highly unlikely.

   ....

   ii It <u>gave way</u> as I pushed it.

   ....

   iii He <u>stopped briefly before entering the room</u> and listened carefully.

   ....

   iv He felt an <u>abrupt impulse</u> to run away as quickly as possible.

   ....

b Explain, in your own words, what the writer means by each of the underlined words and the effect that is achieved by their use:

'Perhaps all of these, or other things, happened together, for all my senses were <u>bewildered</u> all at once and could give me no explanation. The fingers of my right hand, <u>thrust</u> in the opening in the floor, had closed <u>mechanically</u>, found nothing at all, and came up again empty.'

   • ....

   ....

Practice exercises

- ....

....

- ....

....

c Explain, in your own words, how the underlined phrases are used by the writer to suggest the character of the speaker:

'Perhaps all of these, or other things, happened together, for all my senses were <u>bewildered all at once</u> and could give me no explanation. The fingers of my right hand, <u>thrust in the opening in the floor</u>, had <u>closed mechanically, found nothing at all</u>, and came up again empty.'

- ....

....

- ....

....

- ....

....

d Re-read the passage and then **identify** four powerful words or groups of words that suggest the atmosphere both in and outside the house and the thoughts and feelings of the narrator. Your choices should include imagery. **Explain** how each of your chosen words or groups of words is used in the context of the passage.

....

....

....

....

....

....

1 READING

Exercise 6

Witness to paradise being lost: my year in the dying Amazon

By Jonathan Watts

I thought it was a blood moon at first. The dark orange glow appeared at dusk on the far side of the shimmering silver band that is the Xingu River. It was just before 8pm, after the parrots had squawked back to their nests and the insects and frogs were noisily starting the forest nightshift. A flash of lightning from a cloud appeared above almost the same location but the rest of the sky was clear. How could there be a storm? I peered more intently and took a photograph that I could magnify. And there was the answer – a fire, which grew fiercer as I watched, the flames spreading sideways and upwards, flickering red and yellow, billowing smoke into the sky, sparking flashes of lightning every couple of minutes.

I felt sick to the stomach. The Amazon rainforest was being destroyed in front of my eyes. I have been writing about the climate crisis for 16 years, always with a sense of horror but until now, mostly with a sense of distance. This was the first time I had seen it from my home, and it was stranger than I expected. I had not realised until that moment that fire can create its own lightning storms, by creating *pyrocumulonimbus*, which scientists describe as 'the fire-breathing dragon of clouds'.

There was no immediate danger – the fire was several miles away on the other side of one of the world's biggest rivers – but it felt personal. More than 90 per cent of fires in the Amazon are started deliberately to clear trees so the land can be used for cattle ranching or crop cultivation. That meant this arson attack against nature was almost certainly carried out by one of my neighbours. I knew it was probably illegal and that, according to climate science, it would nudge the world's biggest rainforest that much closer to an irreversible tipping point. But there was nothing I could do except watch. The chances of anyone else lifting a finger were next to zero.

The next morning, I learned there were several fires in the rainforest that night. In fact, this was one of the most devastating nights for the Amazon in a decade. Landowners and land-grabbers were rushing to burn with impunity fearing that a change of government policy might stop such indiscriminately started fires. August, September and October were months of fire, a human-made season wedged between the driest point of summer and the onset of the winter monsoons. A haze of charred vegetation shrouded many parts of the rainforest for weeks. My asthma returned for the first time in nine months. Viewed from the forest, arguments far away in parliament about tax rises and government spending were irrelevant; this was life or death.

Adapted from The Guardian, *16 December 2022*

Practice exercises

1 a Identify a word or phrase from the text which suggests the same idea as the words underlined:

  i The explorer had reached <u>the stage where he had no choice;</u> he just had to keep going forward.

  ....

  ii 'It doesn't matter who you are,' said the principal. 'You cannot break the rules <u>without being punished</u>.'

  ....

b Explain, in your own words, what the writer means by each of the words underlined:

'I thought it was a blood moon at first. The dark orange glow appeared at dusk on the far side of the <u>shimmering</u> silver band that is the Xingu River. It was just before 8pm, after the parrots had <u>squawked</u> back to their nests and the insects and frogs were noisily starting the forest <u>nightshift</u>. A flash of lightning from a cloud appeared above almost the same location but the rest of the sky was clear. How could there be a storm?'

- ....

- ....

- ....

c Use one example from the text below to explain how the writer uses language to suggest the fierce, rapid spread of the storm. Use your own words in your explanation.

'a fire, which grew fiercer as I watched, the flames spreading sideways and upwards, flickering red and yellow, billowing smoke into the sky, sparking flashes of lightning every couple of minutes.'

....

....

....

....

d Choose three powerful words or groups of words from the extract below to analyse how the writer uses language to describe his feelings about the fires and their effects on the surroundings.

'Landowners and land-grabbers were rushing to burn with impunity fearing that a change of government policy might stop such indiscriminately started fires. August, September and October were months of fire, a human-made season wedged between the driest point of summer and

1 READING

the onset of the winter monsoons. A haze of charred vegetation shrouded many parts of the rainforest for weeks. My asthma returned for the first time in nine months. Viewed from the forest, arguments far away in parliament about tax rises and government spending were irrelevant; this was life or death.'

....

....

....

....

....

Exercise 7

Bosnian pyramids: fact or fiction?

When they hear the word 'pyramid' most people will think either of the structures built by the ancient Egyptians, the earliest of which was built about 3800 BCE, or perhaps of those built by the Maya in Mexico about 2000 years later. These are both well-known tourist attractions.

A far smaller number of people, however, would associate the word with the landscape round Visoko in the north of Bosnia – a region which is not high on tourists' itineraries. Nevertheless, for people like Semir Osmanagić, the hills in this area are actually the largest man-made pyramids on Earth. As a result of his excavations over the best part of 20 years, Osmanagić has promoted these hills as pyramids built about 35 000 years ago by the Illyrians, an ancient Balkan community. He propounds a theory that the hills are connected by man-made tunnels of a similar period, and are influenced by 'standing waves' from the top of the highest hill which, travelling at the speed of light, are a means of intergalactic communication.

This epiphany of Mr Osmanagić's also reflects another theory he holds that the ancestors of the Mayans came originally from the Pleiades in outer space. 'Ancient peoples built a machine with which they could communicate with the furthest reaches of the cosmos,' he postulated in an interview, and went on to extol the health benefits of visiting the pyramids, claiming that they could reduce high blood pressure and help treat diabetes.

After Mr Osmanagić's theories were published they found a surprisingly receptive audience and there has been a frenzy of visitor activity in the Visoko region. He has now established an archaeological park, Bosnian Pyramid of the Sun Foundation, which is conducting further investigation of the site and provides funds for the development of the site as a tourist attraction promoting 'Bosnian heritage'.

He has certainly had some success in doing this as over 400 000 people have visited the site in the last 20 years, where they have found souvenir stores peddling such items as T-shirts with pyramid logos, and food stalls serving food on pyramid-shaped plates. The park has also

Practice exercises

→ attracted considerable media interest although one investigation using thermal imaging suggested that 'apparently' man-made, concrete blocks were found beneath the valley, which could cast doubt on some of Mr Osmanagić's theories.

Perhaps not surprisingly, not everyone is convinced of the authenticity of the pyramid theory. Mr Osmanagić holds a degree in International Economics but his academic archaeological qualifications are somewhat on the light side and some scientists dispute his findings, claiming that this is an example of pseudo-archaeology intended to create and promote the area in order to boost the local economy, and is a cruel hoax on the unsuspecting public. In their view, the hills are simply natural geological features known as flatirons, which can be found throughout the world.

'What he's found isn't even unusual or spectacular from the geological point of view,' said a geologist from Boston University who spent ten days researching at Visoko. 'It's completely straightforward and mundane.'

1 a Identify a word or phrase from the text which suggests the same idea as the words underlined:

  i 'Before leaving for her holiday, she made a <u>detailed list</u> in order of the places she planned to visit.'

  ....

  ii 'After cudgelling my brains for what seemed hours, I experienced <u>a sudden realisation</u> as to how to solve quadratic equations!'

  ....

b Explain, in your own words, what the writer means by each of the words underlined:

'Nevertheless, for people like Semir Osmanagić, the hills in this area are actually the largest man-made pyramids on Earth. As a result of his excavations over the best part of 20 years, Osmanagić has <u>promoted</u> these hills as pyramids built about 35 000 years ago by the Illyrians, an ancient Balkan community. He <u>propounds</u> a theory that the hills are connected by man-made tunnels of a similar period and are influenced by 'standing waves' from the top of the highest hill which, travelling at the speed of light, are a means of <u>intergalactic</u> communication.'

  • ....

  • ....

  • ....

c Use one example from the text below to explain how the writer uses language to suggest that they are not entirely supportive of Mr Osmanagić's claims about the pyramids. Use your own words in your explanation.

'Perhaps not surprisingly, not everyone is convinced of the authenticity of the pyramid theory. Mr Osmanagić holds a degree in International Economics but his academic archaeological qualifications are somewhat on the light side and some scientists dispute his findings, claiming that this is an example of pseudo-archaeology …'

....

1 READING

....

....

d Choose three powerful words or groups of words from the extract below to analyse how the writer uses language to describe his suspicions and concerns about the claims made by Mr Osmanagić.

'Perhaps not surprisingly, not everyone is convinced of the authenticity of the pyramid theory. Mr Osmanagić holds a degree in International Economics but his academic archaeological qualifications are somewhat on the light side and some scientists dispute his findings, claiming that this is an example of pseudo-archaeology intended to promote the area in order to boost the local economy, and is a cruel hoax on the unsuspecting public. In their view, the hills are simply natural geological features known as flatirons, which can be found throughout the world.

'What he's found isn't even unusual or spectacular from the geological point of view,' said a geologist from Boston University who spent ten days researching at Visoko. 'It's completely straightforward and mundane.'

....

....

....

....

....

....

Exercise 8

This passage is an extract from a short story entitled 'The Scream', which describes the feelings of a young girl, Anna, during a ride on a roller-coaster. Answer the questions that follow.

The front car gave a lurch forwards, and the five other cars followed jerkily. Anna was strapped helplessly to the seat, and paralysed by fear, unable to twist her head or do anything except seal her eyes shut against the red lights fading behind her as the roller-coaster advanced into the tunnel.

At first it was like being on a train. The rocking motion of the car over the uneven track, and the rhythmic pounding against the underside of the car. She felt like a baby being rocked to sleep with the approach of night and the enveloping blackness of the tunnel. Feeling the sudden warmth of the sun on her chilled limbs, Anna became aware that they had emerged into the daylight, and were now slowly ascending a steep section of the course. The car was tipped at such an angle, Anna lay almost horizontally against the back of her seat. She prayed for the climb to go on and on, never reaching its peak so that she would not have to suffer the speedy descent. She was rigid with terror at the very thought of it.

Anna felt the car teetering on the brink at the high point of the track, sure they would either tumble backwards or forwards, she snapped open her eyes for a split second, long enough to see the two silver runners of the

→

Practice exercises

→ track sliding down the other side of the mountain, before her breath was torn from her lungs along with the forming scream which fizzled to nothing, as they plunged head first towards the ground.

It was not a straight drop. There was a violent bend in the track half way down and Anna was thrown sideways against the protective metal bar as the car swung round into a corkscrew spin, winding down, down, only to level out literally metres above the concrete.

Anna gulped in air and the car began to rise again, a ceiling of azure sky visible behind the black frame. She could hear the creak of the cable pulling the car against the gravity, straining with the tension. Please don't let it break, her mind called out. Plummeting down the other side, she became conscious of the deafening shrieks and cries from the cars behind her. One person screamed and the others copied, one by one like falling dominoes, cries of mock horror and pretend fear. Anna's fear was real, embedded deep inside her like an icicle in her heart. She was suffocating, incapable of taking in oxygen with the scream wedged in her throat. The roller-coaster pulled out of its dive and into the first loop, Anna hanging disorientated the wrong way up, her legs jammed into the metal bar, the blood rushing to her head. There was hardly time to catch her breath before the roller-coaster launched into the second, moving faster and faster, the world spinning, dizzy. The third and final loop rushed by; Anna barely noticed – to her they seemed to all run into one horrific spiral.

The chain of golden cars were going up again for the last time, unhurried, creeping inch by inch. Hurry, pleaded Anna to herself, get it over with, let me die soon. She was filled with apprehension, dreading the near vertical drop. High in the air, Anna could see the entire expanse of the theme park spread out beneath, miniature people scurrying from place to place like hungry insects. She saw the tiny camera half hidden at the top, and the faint flash as she sped past it, already on her way to the bottom. The wind flew past her ears, catching hold of her hair and making it stand out behind. Her stomach left her body, suspended in the air as she proceeded on without it. Her fear abandoned her and at last she could scream, as loudly as was possible, the rest of the way down.

From 'The Scream' by H. Briscoe

1 a **Identify** a word or phrase from the text which conveys the same idea as the underlined words:

  i Kim's first driving lesson began as the car took off with a <u>jerk</u>.

  ....

  ii His father in the passenger seat was <u>so frightened he could not move</u>.

  ....

  iii With his heart <u>hammering</u> against his chest, Kim tried again.

  ....

  iv His father felt the car <u>falling sharply out of control</u>.

  ....

 b **Explain**, in your own words, what the writer means by each of the underlined words:

  'Anna's fear was real, <u>embedded</u> deep inside her like an icicle in her heart. She was suffocating, <u>incapable</u> of taking in oxygen with the scream wedged in her throat. The roller-coaster pulled out of its dive and into the first loop, Anna hanging <u>disorientated</u> the wrong way up, her legs jammed into the metal bar,'

1 READING

- ....
- ....
- ....

c **Explain**, in your own words, how the underlined phrases are used by the writer to suggest Anna's experience during the roller-coaster ride:

'Anna's fear was real, <u>embedded deep inside her like an icicle in her heart</u>. She was <u>suffocating, incapable of taking in oxygen with the scream wedged in her throat</u>. The roller-coaster pulled out of its dive and into the first loop, <u>Anna hanging disorientated the wrong way up, her legs jammed into the metal bar,</u>'

....

....

....

....

d Choose three powerful words or groups of words from the extract below to analyse how the writer uses language to describe fear and a sense of terror while on the roller-coaster.

'Anna's fear was real, embedded deep inside her like an icicle in her heart. She was suffocating, incapable of taking in oxygen with the scream wedged in her throat. The roller-coaster pulled out of its dive and into the first loop, Anna hanging disorientated the wrong way up, her legs jammed into the metal bar, the blood rushing to her head. There was hardly time to catch her breath before the roller-coaster launched into the second, moving faster and faster, the world spinning, dizzy. The third and final loop rushed by; Anna barely noticed – to her they seemed to all run into one horrific spiral.'

....

....

....

....

....

Practice exercises

Exercise 9

This is a further extract from the article about the North-west Passage by Sarah Barrell that you came across earlier in this workbook. In the following paragraphs, the writer describes her experience of swimming in the cold Arctic waters and the wildlife that is found there. Answer the questions that follow.

> During the day, when landings allow, those of us holding out for the big mammal show – polar bears, caribou and humorously hirsute musk ox – take hopeful walks along unmapped beaches, guarded by armed crew strategically stationed on higher ground. But on rocky hillsides we mostly unearth the smaller of the Arctic species: miniature meadows of shimmering cotton grass, tiny forests of Arctic willow. 'You're walking in the tree tops!' beams the ship's botanist, Liz Bradfield, as we trot unseeing past the heroic fauna that stands no more than 3 centimetres above the harsh tundra. It's easy to work up a heat walking in five layers of thermal clothing. Bit by bit, layers are peeled off until, one sunny day, a much-vaunted 'polar bear' swim is initiated. Those of the crew who don't go in stand by with essential Arctic beach kit: thick towels and a defibrillator.
>
> The water is thick with chunks of ice that dwarf our sizeable Zodiac inflatable boats, and it's just a notch above freezing. I wade in and am out again in agonising seconds, although my feet take 10 minutes to stop throbbing. Daniel Scott, a more hardy soul, goes in with mask and snorkel. As does the ship's tireless marine biologist, Marie-Josee Desbarats, motivated not by the kudos of taking an Arctic plunge but to get a closer look at the near-microscopic creatures submerged in the ice floe.
>
> Bearded seals flop on and off the steaming ice floe, a musk ox is seen grazing on the mossy hillside and, within minutes, finally, polar bears have been spotted. A mother and baby bear, agile as mountain goats, come down a steep rock face, settling on the beach to watch us bob around on the Zodiacs just offshore. For at least 15 minutes we observe one another, our group more open-mouthed than theirs, before they trot casually back up the cliff.
>
> During the next few days we would all be staggered by such close encounters with wildlife. One afternoon we get within near-petting distance of two snoozy Arctic hares that sit at our feet like plump white pillows while we take endless photos. We move off before they do. Another morning before digesting our own breakfast, the Zodiacs get within 10 metres of a narwhal on the shores of Devon Island. He seems as unfazed by us as is the vast musk ox that crosses our path with the nonchalant swagger of a cowboy as we are trekking later that day. 'You can pretty much guarantee that for these animals, this is their first encounter with humans,' says expedition leader Jason Annahatak as we continue on our way around yet another aptly unnamed bay.
>
> Adapted from *The Independent*, 19 September 2010

1 a Identify a word or phrase from the text which conveys the same idea as the underlined words:

   i The guards were <u>positioned judiciously</u> to protect us without their being seen.

   ....

   ii The snow-covered ground was <u>glistening brightly</u> in the sun.

   ....

1 READING

iii The experience of swimming with polar bears was <u>highly recommended</u>.

....

iv The water temperature was only <u>marginally more</u> than I could stand.

....

b Explain, in your own words, what the writer means by each of the underlined words:

'I wade in and am out again in <u>agonising</u> seconds, although my feet take 10 minutes to stop <u>throbbing</u>. Daniel Scott, a more <u>hardy</u> soul, goes in with mask and snorkel. As does the ship's <u>tireless</u> marine biologist, Marie-Josee Desbarats,'

- ....

- ....

- ....

c Explain, in your own words, how the underlined phrases are used by the writer to express the reactions of herself and her companions to the swim in Arctic waters:

'<u>I wade in and am out again in agonising seconds</u>, although <u>my feet take 10 minutes to stop throbbing</u>. <u>Daniel Scott, a more hardy soul, goes in with mask and snorkel. As does the ship's tireless marine biologist</u>, Marie-Josee Desbarats …'

....

....

....

....

d Choose three powerful words or groups of words from the extract below to analyse how the writer uses language to convey the writer's impressions and feelings about the living creatures that she came across during her time in the Arctic.

'Bearded seals flop on and off the steaming ice floe, a musk ox is seen grazing on the mossy hillside and, within minutes, finally, polar bears have been spotted. A mother and baby bear, agile as mountain goats, come down a steep rock face, settling on the beach to watch us bob around on the Zodiacs just offshore. For at least 15 minutes we observe one another, our group more open-mouthed than theirs, before they trot casually back up the cliff.

During the next few days we would all be staggered by such close encounters with wildlife. One afternoon we get within near-petting distance of two snoozy Arctic hares that sit at our feet like plump white pillows while we take endless photos. We move off before they do.'

....

Exercise 10

Eating on the floor has reminded me of the importance of family time beyond the holidays

By Isma Ishtiaq

One of my favourite childhood memories is family dinners seated cross-legged on a small beige mat. The sun was often setting, casting a warm amber glow through the curtains. We'd have a delicious Pakistani meal — the centrepiece was often a steaming pot of biryani decorated with strands of saffron, its spiced aroma filling the air. On other occasions, it would be a creamy butter chicken and homemade naan. We sat in a circle, passing plates, telling stories and sharing highlights from our day. This was a long-standing tradition that my father passed on from his childhood growing up in the bustling city of Lahore to mine in the quiet suburbs of north Delta in B.C.

Dad often emphasized that it wasn't just about sharing a meal, but that sitting on the ground to eat together was a humbling experience that fostered gratitude for the food we were blessed with. As I sat on that simple woven mat, I realized it was also the beautiful embodiment of the threads that held us together as a family and of celebrating our culture in a way that transcended generations.

But as years passed, my siblings and I grew up and got too busy to make it to those family dinners. Between work, school and sports, the time to sit together was no longer there and soon more than a decade lapsed since we had sat on that beige mat.

It wasn't until a Thanksgiving dinner, when I was 23, that I thought again of our childhood family tradition of eating dinner together on the ground. I invited my friends to spend Thanksgiving with my family at my house, and told them about this tradition. My friends, all of different cultural backgrounds from my own, were intrigued by the idea and asked if they could try it out.

I rummaged through the storage closet and found, to my surprise, the same beige mat, now rugged and worn-out. My friends didn't seem to mind the humble state of it. So I gave it a shake and laid it out on the living room floor. We recreated the familiar circle on the ground, placing our plates full of Thanksgiving turkey in front of us.

What happened that night was a beautiful moment. My father looked over at me from where he was eating at the dining table, smiled and joined us. As he explained the tradition to my friends,

1 READING

the rest of the parents – still at the dinner table – watched curiously as we revelled in the simplicity of togetherness. Most of my friends said they enjoyed the experience. One of them said it reminded her of sitting around a campfire!

This was the moment that bridged the gap between the traditions of my heritage and the customs of our home in Canada.

The next evening, my siblings, mom and I arranged the Tupperware containers of leftovers from the night before onto the dining table. We waited for my dad to arrive home from work, and took our seats. My dad walked down the stairs, the beige cloth peeking out from under his arm. Smiling, he looked at me and spread it on the ground.

Inspired by our Thanksgiving dinner, he decided to resurrect the tradition.

Once again, we began to share food and stories on that mat. We rediscovered its ability to bring us closer, despite the demands of our busy lives. It was a reminder that the simple act of sharing stories, passing plates and gathering together could weave the threads of my family even tighter.

These days, as the sun sets and casts a warm, amber glow through the curtains, we find ourselves sitting on the same beige mat with a mosaic of food before us. We make a collective effort to prioritize dinner time. It has become a sacred time to set aside our individual concerns and truly be together. Some days, the woven mat is replaced by a dining table for more formal family gatherings, but the essence of togetherness remains the same — not just on Thanksgiving but during the holiday season and all year long. Just as it did in my father's childhood, and just as it would do for generations to come.

From www.cbc.ca/news/canada/first-person-eat-on-the-floor-1.7066027

1 a Identify a word or phrase from the text which conveys the same idea as the underlined words:

   i The <u>pleasantly piquant smell</u> of my mother's cooking welcomed me as I came in from school.

   ....

   ii The food was delicious and <u>encouraged my thanks</u> to my mother.

   ....

   iii The ancient temple was the <u>living expression</u> of my country's past.

   ....

   iv In its silent beauty, the building <u>surpassed</u> all those that had been built in later times.

   ....

   b Explain, in your own words, what the writer means by each of the underlined words:

   'Dad often <u>emphasized</u> that it wasn't just about sharing a meal, but that sitting on the ground to eat together was a <u>humbling</u> experience that fostered gratitude for the food we were blessed

Practice exercises

with. As I sat on that simple woven mat, I realized it was also the beautiful embodiment of the threads that held us together as a family and of <u>celebrating our culture</u> in a way that transcended generations.'

- ....
- ....
- ....

c **Explain**, in your own words, how the underlined phrases are used by the writer to express her own and her friends' thoughts and feelings about the family meals:

'But as years passed, my siblings and I <u>grew up and got too busy</u> to make it to those family dinners. Between work, school and sports, the time to sit together was no longer there and soon more <u>than a decade lapsed</u> since we had sat on that beige mat.

It wasn't until a Thanksgiving dinner, when I was 23, that I thought again of our childhood family tradition of eating dinner together on the ground. I invited my friends to spend Thanksgiving with my family at my house, and told them about this tradition. My friends, all of different cultural backgrounds from my own, were <u>intrigued by the idea</u> and asked if they could try it out.'

....

....

....

....

....

d Choose three powerful words or groups of words from paragraphs 5–7 ('I rummaged ...' to '... in Canada') to analyse how the writer uses language to convey her appreciation of the importance of such gatherings of family and friends.

....

....

....

....

Photocopying prohibited   Cambridge IGCSE™ First Language English Workbook 3rd Edition   33

2 Directed writing

Student book, Units 7 and 10

Other ways of testing your reading skills are questions that ask you to write at length in response to a passage that you have read. Some questions will ask for an extended response to reading and expect you to build on your understanding of the passage that you have read through producing a descriptive or narrative piece of writing. Other questions will require a discursive or argumentative treatment of key points from the source passage and involve a more critical, evaluative consideration of its content. Remember that these questions test both your reading and writing skills.

It is important that you spend a considerable part of your time on reading to ensure that you have understood the passage as fully as you can. You should try to keep your answers to about 200–250 words – if you try to write too much, it is extremely likely that your answer will be unfocused and contain errors of expression caused by carelessness and haste.

> **Key point**
>
> All directed writing tasks will give you an audience and a context for your writing. It is important that, as far as possible, you use a register in your writing that is suitable for the audience.
>
> If the task requires you to write a continuation or development of the story in the stimulus passage, and you write in a style similar to that of the original passage, you will have shown that you have appreciated the language of the writer and you should be credited for this.

Extended response to reading exercises

The practice exercises on the following pages provide you with tasks to practise your skills in building on the content and ideas of a reading passage. (Some of the passages are the same as those in Section 1 to provide practice in answering short-answer comprehension questions. You might like to start by answering these as the work you have already done in answering the comprehension questions should help you in writing your answers.)

> **Note**
>
> In the following exercises, there are two or three questions set on each passage to provide you with practice for this type of question. However, remember that in the examination only one directed writing question will be set on the reading passage.
>
> For each practice question, you should base your response on what you have read in the passage but you should not copy from it. You should attempt to use your own words throughout. Your answer should address and develop all three points in the question.

Exercise 1

Read carefully the following extract from the article about the North-west Passage by Sarah Barrell. Then answer the questions that follow.

The North-west Passage: A 21st-century expedition

By Sarah Barrell

A cruise, led by Inuit people, follows the early explorers around the Canadian Arctic in waters that are still largely uncharted. Sarah Barrell went aboard.

Summer in the Arctic and dust, not snow, covers the ground. In Gjoa Haven, an Inuit settlement on King William, an island in the heart of the North-west Passage, there's dust on the seats of skidoos. Dust, too, on the coats of the scrappy sled dogs that are tethered in long lines waiting for winter and starter's orders.

→

Extended response to reading exercises

About them, teenagers charge around on battered all-terrain vehicles, kicking up more dust, making the most of the light evenings and the comparatively balmy 10 °C temperatures. It's hard to imagine amid all this, with the sun shooting in laser-bright arcs off the town's tin-roofed houses, that somewhere in or around this island, Sir John Franklin, an intrepid 19th-century Arctic explorer, met a dark and icy end trying to discover the fabled North-west Passage.

He vanished more than a century and a half ago, but the fever to find the remains of Franklin's expedition still runs high in the remote Canadian Arctic, some 5000 kilometres from the shores of the UK. Earlier this summer, Canadian authorities unveiled the wreck of HMS *Investigator*, one of the many doomed 19th-century rescue ships sent in search of Franklin's expedition. Then, just last week in the town of Gjoa Haven itself, archaeologists unearthed what could be the Holy Grail of Arctic exploration history. At the behest of local brothers Wally and Andrew Porter, a box was excavated containing, the Porters claim, long sought-after records from the ill-fated Franklin expedition that might reveal its final whereabouts.

Franklin was more advanced in age and overweight than other explorers of his era; his ships were also spectacularly over-burdened when he left for his third Arctic expedition in 1845. The British Admiralty brushed this aside as the fervour to conquer the North-west Passage once again reached a peak. There was prize money at stake (£20,000 [USD 28,000] offered by the British crown) for anyone who could navigate the elusive, icy waterway connecting the Atlantic and Pacific oceans. But beyond this, there was the chance to forge crucial northern trade links between Europe and Asia, one that would open up a new route to the spice lands and, in addition, avoid stormy sailings around Cape Horn. But was Franklin the man to fly Britain's flag into the uncharted north?

Probably not, given that he had survived his first expedition charting Canada's Arctic coast by eating his own boots and being rescued by Native Americans. There was much that European explorers could learn from the three centuries of sailors who had battled to find a northerly route connecting the Atlantic and Pacific – in short, to travel light and use local expertise. Instead, highlighting the egotism of the time, Franklin's expedition sailed out of London laden with chests of fine china, dead-weight sledges and canned food that would later finish them off with lead-poisoning. After three winters trapped in ice, Franklin's crew abandoned their two ships, the *Erebus* and *Terror*, somewhere off the coast of King William Island and were never seen again.

I manage to stop at this remote part of the Arctic Archipelago on board an eight-day tour, uniquely led by a local Inuit team. In true expedition style, there are no promised ports of call as conditions can change suddenly. Our first two days' passage is devoid of ice or high seas, but we hear that another cruise ship has run aground in shallow straits to the far west. 'Even with the ice receding, there's only been clear passage here for about five years,' says Dugald Wells, President of Cruise North, a former marine engineer who has been working in the Arctic since the mid-1980s. 'I came up here because it was fun – a real frontier. It still is, but you have to respect the fact that only 50 per cent of these waters are surveyed,' he says.

Adapted from *The Independent*, 19 September 2010

2 DIRECTED WRITING

1. Imagine that you are Sarah Barrell, the writer of this article. On your return from your trip, you have been invited to give a talk to a group of Cambridge IGCSE students at a school in your home town. Write the words of your talk. You should include:

   - information about Franklin and the search for the North-west Passage

   - details of the area of the Arctic that you visited

   - what you found particularly interesting and enjoyable about your trip and why you recommend people in your audience to visit the area at some point in their lives.

   Continue writing on a separate sheet of paper if necessary.

Extended response to reading exercises

2 On her return from her visit to the Arctic, Sarah Barrell is interviewed on a local radio station about her experiences. Write the words of the conversation between Sarah and the interviewer. The interviewer asks these three main questions during the course of the interview:

- Tell me about Sir John Franklin and your interest in his journey.
- Were there any other reasons for your visit to the Arctic?
- What did you learn from your trip?

Continue writing on a separate sheet of paper if necessary.

2 DIRECTED WRITING

Exercise 2

In the following blog post, Aditi Chawla gives an account of a memorable encounter while researching the animal population of the Great Himalayan National Park. Read the extract and then answer the questions that follow.

An unexpected encounter

By Aditi Chawla

It was spring when we visited the Great Himalayan National Park in Himachal Pradesh, a UNESCO World Heritage Site in the far Western Himalayas. It had been a cold, snowy winter and feeling the gentle warmth in the air, seeing the blossoms, filled us with excitement and optimism about the trip ahead. We paused before the entrance to extend our greetings to GB's Hippo. Sadly, the hippo is really no more than a large sedentary bolder but, sat as he was at the bottom of a small waterfall, it was easy to convince ourselves that he had just dunked his head under the water momentarily and would soon raise it to look at us. As we set off, the sound of the Tirthan River echoed around us, its waters swollen with the receding snow of early spring. Only as we ventured deeper into the forest was it drowned out by the howling of the wind. The beauty of the place distracted me, and I lagged behind my companions and our guide, Kabir, only catching up when we arrived at a diversion point.

We were visiting the park as part of our research and had been given permission by the National Mission on Himalayan Studies (NMHS) and the Wildlife Institute of India to enter some parts not normally accessible to visitors. Crossing an old wooden bridge, we found ourselves at the beginning of a natural path which seemed to have been formed by the movement of animals heading down to a point on the river which was easy to cross. It was here that we set our first camera trap, a movement-sensitive device which allowed us to capture images of the wildlife with little human interference. With this work done, we headed uphill, aware of the weight of our packs on our backs, as we reminded ourselves that it was the park's wide range of elevation which was in part responsible for its beautiful and diverse plant life.

The ascent took us into thick oak forest. Sometimes we could hear the Tirthan but at other times the sound seemed unable to penetrate the thick vegetation around us. For some of the way we had chatted in quiet voices, talking about our work or pointing out interesting vegetation, but soon the trek became too difficult and we fell silent. Perhaps taking this as his cue, Kabir suggested that we catch our breaths and have the meals that we had packed, and we looked around us, waiting for him to advise whether it was a good place to stop. All around were patches of freshly dug-up earth. 'Bhalu,' Kabir said, the Hindi word for bear. It was evidence of bears searching for insects and mites, he said, adding that this part of the forest was a good place for sighting the endangered Himalayan Brown Bear.

And then, as if his voice had called it into existence, there before us was an adult Himalayan Brown Bear, at work on the ground, using its long claws to dig through the earth. We all froze, with the animal no less than 20m away. We'd stopped to catch our breath but now we stood holding our breaths as the animal sensed our presence and stood to face us. Its nostrils flared and it seemed to look me directly in the eye. Had the bear been with a cub, it might have charged us and our story would have had a different ending, but instead it turned and sprinted off, surprisingly agile given its large size. We watched its beautiful golden-brown body disappear into the trees.

For a moment we remained frozen until Kabir, pointing to the equipment that we carried on our backs, said, 'So many cameras, no picture.' We all laughed although it was only then, after the moment of absolute fear was gone that I wondered why I hadn't grabbed at the phone that was hanging on a strap around my neck, and taken a picture. I have on occasion taken a picture to →

Extended response to reading exercises

→
share, of a delicious meal I've been served at a restaurant or something funny that I've seen in a shop. But the day I came face to face with the endangered Himalayan Brown Bear I didn't think to take a picture!

Once we'd all recovered from our fright, we felt an unexpected sense of elation. There are between 500 and 750 Himalayan Brown Bears left in India and we'd just seen one of them close up. It's not often that you experience something that you know will probably never happen to you again in your life; or something that you know you are one of a very few people to have experienced. We set up a camera trap nearby, so perhaps we will have a picture of our friend in time, but energised by the experience we decided to press on.

Walking through the forest we emerged into a lush meadow full of spring blossoms. From there, across a brook, our campsite came into view. In the hut, Kabir lit a fire and made us cups of tea. Perhaps it was only then that we were able to truly relax, letting go of the suppressed hysteria that had powered us through the walk to the camp. As the sun began to set, we sat on the ground outside of the hut and looked at the warm glow of the butter-coloured sky. I might have felt grateful to be alive and uninjured (and believe me, I was!) but in the twilight I was even more aware of the beauty of the place and most of all felt gratitude for the encounter itself. It's a rare thing to be so close to such a beautiful animal in its natural habitat, and it may be impossible to describe the magic of connecting with a species so different from our own. But it's a reminder of why we must work so hard to protect endangered animals and to preserve habitat, not just for their sake but for our own.

1 After returning from the National Park, Aditi was interviewed by a national newspaper. Imagine that you are the journalist who conducted the interview. Write an article with the headline 'Meeting with a Rare Bear'. In your article you should include:

- what you learned about the purpose of the expedition and the National Park
- how Aditi and her colleagues reacted when the bear appeared
- Aditi's thoughts and feelings about meeting the bear both at the time and afterwards.

Continue writing on a separate sheet of paper if necessary.

....

....

....

....

....

....

2 DIRECTED WRITING

....

....

....

....

....

2 Imagine that you are Aditi. Before you return home after leaving the park, write a letter to your sister who lives in a different country, about your experience. In your letter you should include:

- details of your work and your visit to the National Park
- details of the park, its scenery and its overall atmosphere
- your meeting with the bear and why it was such an important experience for you.

Continue writing on a separate sheet of paper if necessary.

....

....

....

....

....

....

....

....

....

....

....

Extended response to reading exercises

Exercise 3

The following passage is an extract from the short story 'The Country of the Blind' by H.G. Wells. Nunez, an explorer in the Andes mountain range in South America, has fallen down a mountainside onto a rocky ledge where he has spent the night. Read the passage carefully and then answer the questions that follow.

He was awakened by the singing of birds in the trees far below. He sat up and perceived he was at the foot of a vast precipice. Over against him another wall of rock reared itself against the sky. The gorge between these precipices ran east and west. It was full of the morning sunlight, which lit the mass of fallen mountain to the west. Below him it seemed there was a precipice equally steep, but behind the snow in the gully he found a sort of chimney-cleft dripping with snow-water, down which a desperate man might venture. He found it easier than it seemed and after a rock climb of no particular difficulty came to a steep slope of trees.

He turned his face up the gorge and saw it opened out above onto green meadows, among which he glimpsed a cluster of stone huts of unfamiliar fashion. At times his progress was like clambering along the face of a wall, and after a time the rising sun ceased to strike along the gorge, the voices of the singing birds died away, and the air grew cold and dark about him. But the distant valley with its houses was all the brighter for that. Among the rocks he noted an unfamiliar fern. He picked a frond or so and gnawed its stalk, and found it helpful.

About midday he came at last out of the gorge into the plain and the sunlight. He was stiff and weary; he sat down in the shadow of a rock, filled up his flask with water from a spring and drank it down. He remained for a time, resting before he went on to the houses.

They were very strange to his eyes, and indeed the whole appearance of that valley became, as he regarded it, stranger and more unfamiliar. The greater part of its surface was lush green meadow, starred with many beautiful flowers. It was irrigated with extraordinary care, and showed signs of systematic farming. High up and ringing the valley about was a wall, and what appeared to be a water channel, from which the little trickles of water that fed the meadow plants came. On the higher slopes flocks of llamas cropped the scanty grass. The irrigation streams ran together into a main channel down the centre of the valley, and this was enclosed on either side by a wall chest high. A number of paths paved with black and white stones, and each with a curious little kerb at the side, ran here and there in an orderly manner.

The houses of the central village were quite unlike those of the mountain villages he knew. They stood in a continuous row on either side of a central street of astonishing cleanness. Here and there their walls were pierced by a door, but not a solitary window broke their even frontage. They were parti-coloured with extraordinary irregularity, smeared with a sort of plaster that was sometimes grey, sometimes drab, sometimes slate-coloured or dark brown. It was the sight of this wild plastering that made the explorer say to himself, 'The good man who did that must have been as blind as a bat.'

He descended a steep place, and so came to the wall and channel that ran about the valley. He could now see a number of men and women resting on piled heaps of grass, as if taking a siesta, in the remoter part of the meadow. Nearer the village a number of children were lying on their backs, and then coming closer to him he saw three men. These men wore garments of llama cloth and boots and belts of leather, and caps of cloth with back and ear flaps. They followed one another in single file, walking slowly and yawning as they walked, like men who have been up all night. There was something so reassuringly prosperous and respectable in their bearing that after a moment's hesitation Nunez stood forward as conspicuously as possible upon his rock, and gave vent to a mighty shout that echoed round the valley.

From 'The Country of the Blind' by H.G. Wells

2 DIRECTED WRITING

1. Imagine that you are Nunez. It is the day after the events described in the passage. You are now resting in the village and writing up the events of the previous days in your journal. In your journal entry you should include:

   - an account of how you came to find the valley and the village
   - what your first impressions of the village were
   - what happened after you entered the village and met the inhabitants.

   Continue writing on a separate sheet of paper if necessary.

Extended response to reading exercises

2 You are a journalist working for the magazine *Travellers' Tales*. A man called Nunez has contacted you and said that he has just returned from an unusual experience in the Andes. You interview him and then write an account of his experiences for the magazine. Your article is entitled 'Secrets of the Hidden Village' and it should include:

- information about Nunez and a description of his character
- details of how he discovered the village
- what he told you about the people he met and the time he spent with them.

Continue writing on a separate sheet of paper if necessary.

2 DIRECTED WRITING

Exercise 4

The following article is about the apparent sightings of mysterious creatures around the world. Read the article and then answer the questions that follow.

Now you see them, now you don't; do yetis really exist?

Shakespeare's Hamlet tells his friend, Horatio, that there are 'more things in Heaven and Earth than are dreamt of in your philosophy' and, despite our living over 400 years since these words were written, we can't deny that they still have some truth.

How else can we make sense of the ongoing accounts of apparent sightings of strange and unknown beings inhabiting the more unexplored areas of our planet? To name just a few, people claim to have seen creatures such as Bigfoot (also known as Sasquatch) in the more remote forest areas of the north-west USA; a hairy, human-like giant, the Wild Man, has been reported in the Dolomites, a mountain area in north-eastern Italy; and Scotland's Loch Ness has its monster, a huge serpent-like prehistoric being that occasionally appears to boatmen. Perhaps the most persistently-reported creatures are the yeti, or Abominable Snowmen, large, ape-like creatures inhabiting remote mountain areas, including the Himalayas.

Some of the most recent appearances of the yeti have been in the isolated Kemerovo region of Siberia where three separate sightings were reported by fishermen. One group of fishermen saw what they thought to be bears on the distant shore. As they drew nearer, they realised the creatures resembled humans and the fishermen called out asking them if they needed help. Rather than replying, the creatures, covered all in fur, turned and rushed away.

Another sighting of a group of similar beings was reported shortly afterwards in the same area. Unfortunately, the fishermen involved could not see them clearly as their binoculars were broken and they had no equipment with which to take photographs, but they claimed the creatures were covered in fur and walked like humans.

There have been reports of similar creatures seen in the vast expanses of Siberia but, as yet, there have been no images recorded to provide evidence of the existence of yetis.

Igor Burtsev, Russia's leading 'yeti' expert, described the sightings as 'significant' and claims that in his view there is a population of at least 30 yetis inhabiting the Kemerovo region. Burtsev has held conferences in Moscow devoted to discussing the existence of yetis in the area and has also led expeditions to search for them. He believes that, as a result of these searches, he has found yeti hair but, as yet, there have been no DNA findings made public. He believes that creatures such as the yeti and Bigfoot are the missing link between the Neanderthals and Homo sapiens. He concludes, 'The descriptions of the habits of the Abominable Snowmen are similar from all over the world.'

Mr Burtsev has strongly denied accusations that yeti 'sightings' are a deliberate ploy to attract tourists to a far-flung region.

Dr John Bindernagel, a biologist working in the same area of Siberia, has also suggested that experts exploring there may have come across a yeti nest. They reported trees twisted forcefully to form an arch in a way that was unlikely to have been done by a human or other mammal. Trees twisted in a similar way have been found in North America and have given rise to the theory that Bigfoot makes nests.

Extended response to reading exercises

> Other sightings of bulky, 7-foot-tall bear-like creatures walking on their hind legs have been reported in France as well as the Himalayas and North America but, according to Dr Bindernagel, many scientists are unwilling to investigate these as they are deterred by 'jokes and taboos'.
>
> ## A little more about the yeti
>
> In the 19th century, Buddhist monks living in the Himalayas were the first to record the possible existence of yetis. They described a strange creature similar to an ape, carrying a large rock for protection and making a whistling sound as it moved.
>
> People's interest in the possible existence of yetis increased during the 20th century when visitors to remote mountainous areas began making explorations either to try to capture a yeti or, at least, to capture one on camera. Although not successful, they did report seeing strange markings in the snow. An expedition to the Everest region, organised by a national UK newspaper in 1954, took photographs of ancient paintings of yetis and large footprints in the snow, as well as finding some hair samples believed to be from a yeti scalp. British mountaineer Don Whillans claimed to have seen a yeti-like creature when he was climbing Annapurna in 1970.

1 Imagine that you are Igor Burtsev. You have now had time to study the accounts of both yeti sightings in the Kemerovo region. You have been asked to prepare a report for the other delegates at the Moscow conference. In your report you should refer to:

- what you have learned from the people who witnessed the most recent sightings of the yetis
- how their accounts are similar to, and different from, earlier accounts of yeti sightings
- your reasons for believing that yetis do exist and reasons why other people might believe that they do not exist.

Continue writing on a separate sheet of paper if necessary.

....

....

....

....

....

....

....

....

2 DIRECTED WRITING

....

....

....

....

....

....

....

....

....

....

....

....

....

2 You are a presenter of a popular science television programme. As part of a feature about unexplained phenomena, you are interviewing John Bindernagel about stories concerning yetis and other similar creatures. Write the words of your conversation. As the interviewer, you ask the following three main questions:

- Could you tell the viewers about some of the most interesting sightings of yetis and other similar creatures?

- What theories have been developed as to why yetis might exist?

- What reasons do you have for thinking that we should believe or not believe in the existence of yetis?

Continue writing on a separate sheet of paper if necessary.

....

....

2 DIRECTED WRITING

Exercise 5

In the following article, a journalist considers the possible return of airships as a means of transport. Read the extract and then answer the questions that follow.

Are blimps the future?

Taking all factors into account, the commercial aviation industry is responsible for about 5 per cent of greenhouse gas emissions. Environmentalists predict that unless something is done to reduce this, that percentage is likely to double by 2050. The air industry is facing huge pressure from consumers and governing bodies to become more climate-friendly. This is clearly an important issue as more and more people are travelling long distances and flying, despite its many discomforts and inconveniences, is still the fastest and most efficient means of transport.

Much research has gone into finding a solution for this concern and most airlines have considered the possibility of following the lead of the automobile industry and developing aircraft powered by a cleaner from of energy such as electric (or hydrogen) cell technology. Although, in principle, this would seem a possible alternative, there are some serious logistical problems.

First among these is the fact that electric cell batteries are extremely heavy and, to power a plane carrying several hundreds of people and their baggage, would need to be much larger than those used in a family-sized electric car – and, let's not forget, electric cars are not intended to take off into the stratosphere! In addition to this, heavy lithium-ion batteries do not have sufficient charge to power aircraft for long distances, hydrogen cell technology would require too much storage space on board the aircraft, and both methods present fire-risks.

One left-field suggestion which has been put forward for reducing the carbon output of air travel is to consider something from an earlier period of air transport – the airship, or blimp, which could provide a shorter term, green solution to the problem by using and building on previous technology.

A Frenchman, Henri Giffard, developed the first airship in 1852 and made a successful flight in it, fifty years before the Wright brothers made their historic powered flight. During the decades subsequent to Giffard's flight, the German Zeppelin Corporation developed on his ideas and eventually created the world's first commercial airline using Zeppelins (airships) to transport passengers around the world. They provided relaxing and comfortable flights travelling at 128 km (80 miles) per hour with a range of 10 000 km (6250 miles), in the period between the First and Second World Wars. The golden age of airships came to a tragic end, however, when the hydrogen-powered Hindenburg airship (on its 37th transatlantic crossing) burst into flames while landing in New Jersey. As a result, people lost faith in airships as a means of transport and the fixed wing airplane industry soon took its place.

Now, with the development of new technology, modern airship companies such as Hybrid Air Vehicles (HAV) have developed and are hoping to become commercially established. The company's flagship is the Airlander 10. It is a hybrid of a blimp and an airplane. It comprises a flexible body filled with helium (a non-flammable gas) which allows it to lift off the ground, and 'ultra-efficient' combustion engines to move while in the air. It can fly, like the Zeppelins, at 80 mph (128 kph). Although this is much slower than a conventional jet plane, it offers much greater comfort, with ample room for passengers to move around, and floor to ceiling windows to add to the sense of space to see and to think about the future of the world before us, and especially its modes of transport.

Extended response to reading exercises

1 You are taking part in a school debating competition on the topic of conserving energy. You have read the article above and also researched airships online.

Write your speech proposing their commercial use. You should include the following points:

- What airships are and what we know of their history.

- The positives and negatives of using them for transporting people and goods.

- Why you would recommend them as a viable alternative to conventional aircraft.

Continue writing on a separate sheet of paper if necessary.

2 DIRECTED WRITING

2 Imagine you are the journalist who wrote the article above. You have interviewed the Publicity Officer for Hybrid Air Vehicles (HAV) who has tried to convince you of why airships are the future of air travel after your article was published. You have received several letters from your readers who express doubts about the use of airships, however.

Write an account of your interview with the Publicity Officer in which you give details of:

- the Publicity Officer's reasons why airships should be used for commercial transport
- the main concerns raised by your readers and the responses the Publicity Officer gives to them
- your concluding assessment of the points made in the interview and your own thoughts on the matter.

Continue writing on a separate sheet of paper if necessary.

Exercise 6

In the following passage, the writer describes how, while on holiday on a small island in the Hawaiian archipelago, he finally managed to escape from his computer and all the other electronic gadgets that control his life when he is at work. Read the passage and then answer the questions that follow.

Wireless-less

My working life revolves around using technology; nearly everything I do depends on being online and using either my laptop or phone. In some ways, it is convenient as I do not have to go into an office every day and can work from the comfort of my own home, but, nevertheless, I sometimes feel that I am entrapped in the virtual world.

I needed a holiday and an escape from the ever-present pressures of 21st-century life. I took the plunge and organised a fortnight's break, just for myself, in a secret location on an island in the North Pacific. I planned to travel light and, most importantly, to leave electronic devices at home. In case of emergencies while travelling, I took my cell-phone with me but ensured that my accommodation on the island was out of cell-phone range.

On arrival, I rented a car and after driving for several kilometres along red-dirt roads reached the comfortable cottage near the beach that I had rented. I knew that living by a beach would allow me enjoyable opportunities for relaxation. However, while driving to the cottage, I was made aware of how difficult it would be to escape technology entirely. Noisy helicopters full of tourists disturbed the skies above my head; the rumbles of tour boats racing round the island echoed from the surrounding ocean. And even in these remote surroundings I noticed only a short drive from my cottage, a busy internet café.

This was my greatest temptation. I was determined to lie on the beach and not to check my emails. My friends and family could not understand this desire on my part as they knew that in my job I am permanently online and email is central to my daily life. It was as if I was addicted to it – they could not understand how I could live without it and I knew that it would take a great effort to ensure that I did not visit the café for the duration of my stay.

It was night by the time I settled in my cottage and unpacked my few belongings. The black-sand beach and the gently swelling sea, only a few metres from my door, were illuminated by the full moon. The mango trees surrounding the cottage cast complex shadows across my veranda. All I could see were shadowy piles of loose driftwood in irregular heaps along the shore. The only sound was that of the waves calmly whispering; my soul was soothed and I realised that I was able to log-off from my working life.

The next morning I turned to the second part of my plan. The island offered all varieties of beaches and beach activities: wading, body-surfing, swimming and sun-bathing; bodysurfing beaches, wading beaches, secluded beaches with white sand and lined with palm trees. I was free to engage in all kinds of activity. I could hike to nearby villages or even stroll from some hotel into the welcoming waters of the Pacific.

I had guidebooks that could offer me advice but the more I saw of what the island had to offer, the more I started to worry about which options I should take; what would be the most efficient way of making the most of my time? Then it hit me – going to the beach should not be about efficiency; efficiency belongs to the world of email that I was leaving behind. The beach was not about efficiency but provided an exactly opposite lifestyle which I should allow myself to give into.

And so, I finally found myself sitting motionless in my chair in my cottage, my book closed on my lap, idly watching a lizard skitter across the ceiling. That evening, as I watched the sun sinking slowly into the waves, I realised that there was no cause for concern when a gentle shower of rain started to fall. It didn't matter if I was wet or dry – the beach was all that mattered and without electronic reminders, time was non-existent. On the beach I could wait for the coconut to fall; I didn't need to shake the tree.

2 DIRECTED WRITING

1 Imagine that you are the writer. It is the evening of the fifth day of your holiday and you are sitting in your cottage writing your journal. In your journal entry you should include:

- details of what you have spent your time doing while you have been on the island

- what you have found most pleasing about your time on the island and about the island itself

- your thoughts on not using any electronic gadgets and how this might change your outlook when you return to work.

Continue writing on a separate sheet of paper if necessary.

Extended response to reading exercises

2 You are a journalist for the local island newspaper and have recently interviewed the writer during their time on the island. Write an article with the headline 'Making Time Stand Still'. In your article you should include:

- your impressions of the writer as a person and their reasons for visiting the island
- how the writer found life without electronic devices and any problems this caused
- how far the writer feels that the island provided an ideal getaway and whether they think visitors in future will be able to have a similar experience.

Continue writing on a separate sheet of paper if necessary.

2 DIRECTED WRITING

3 Imagine that you are the writer. It has been two days since you first arrived on the island and you realise that your friends will be wondering how you are getting on. Write a letter to one of your friends at work. In your letter you should include:

- your first impressions of the island, what you have been doing since you arrived and what you plan to do for the remainder of your holiday

- how you are coping without email and other electronic devices, and why your friend would benefit from doing something similar

- your thoughts about how long you think the island will remain unspoilt by outside influences.

Continue writing on a separate sheet of paper if necessary.

Directed writing exercises

As mentioned at the start of this section, the directed writing tasks require you to respond by writing in either a discursive or an argumentative way.

Exercise 7

The passage below is the text of a circular letter from an international banking group which was posted on its website as information for its customers. Read it carefully and answer the questions that follow.

WaterAid

Dear Loyal Customer,

You may be interested to hear that as well as managing your personal finances as efficiently as we can, as a major banking company we consider it of ethical importance that we also donate some of our annual profits to deserving causes. This year, we have chosen to support the organisation WaterAid, and we are providing the following information to explain our reasons for doing so.

WaterAid is a non-governmental, non-profit-making organisation, established in 1981. It is focused on water, sanitation and hygiene and currently operates in 34 countries around the world. Its vision is, 'of a world where everyone has access to safe water and sanitation'. It has already helped to improve the lives of nearly 30 million people, but researchers estimate there are a further two billion in need of its assistance. As a company, we fully support WaterAid's objectives, and we hope that you will do too. Their overall principles, like ours, are focused on Health, Education, Diet and Nutrition, and Gender Equality. Please continue to read the following paragraphs and discover further details about WaterAid's work.

Ensuring that people are provided with clean water and sanitation will help greatly in eliminating poverty and will change many families' lives in many countries. Easily accessible clean water and improved sanitation will lead to better health and will, consequently, result in better school and work attendance, increased income for families and individuals, and a far better quality of life for all.

We will ensure that the money we donate will be used by WaterAid to fund specific projects and we will keep you informed of their progress through regular online communications. In fact, you might like to visit WaterAid's own website (www.wateraid.org) where you can read stories about individual people such as Lucy, whose life has been changed by being provided with clean water and sanitation.

You can also discover the range of sustainable technological approaches used by WaterAid – such as rain-water harvesting, protection of spring water sources, sub-surface dams, digging (by hand) of wells and boreholes where needed and improved latrine facilities – which are intended to further their objectives. The website provides more detailed technical details about the methods used to carry out this work. For example, in order to provide clean water to communities, WaterAid will establish boreholes and wells. The wells are sealed to prevent future contamination and will be fitted with pumps. Instruction will be given to people living in the area so that they know how to use and look after them for themselves. Where groundwater is particularly scarce, people will be advised on how to harvest rainwater; sanitation and hygiene education will also be provided to all.

WaterAid is an established charity with over a quarter of a million supporters but more will always be welcome to cater for the needs of a further two billion in need.

2 DIRECTED WRITING

1 You have spent a week of work experience at the company that produced the passage above on their website. You have been convinced of the importance of the work done by WaterAid and support the company's wish to promote this.

You have been chosen to give a talk in school assembly to your year group about your work experience.

In your talk you should explain:

- what WaterAid does and what the charity believes in

- what you learned about why WaterAid's work is important to our present-day world

- why you support its work and how other people in your year group can contribute to it.

Continue writing on a separate sheet of paper if necessary.

Directed writing exercises

2 During your work experience at the company you were required by your teacher to keep a journal of your time with them; you have included some extracts from your journal below. These include:

- what you learned about the company and its support for WaterAid during your time there
- why the company felt it important that they should promote WaterAid's work on a wider scale and how they do this
- your own thoughts about the importance of these ideas and how you can best support them.

Continue writing on a separate sheet of paper if necessary.

2 DIRECTED WRITING

Exercise 8

The article below is from a magazine feature titled 'Have Your Say' in which readers are invited to express their views on matters that are of importance to them.

Veganism and me

Hello, everyone; my name is Kim and I'm a vegan.

I want to tell you about why what I eat every day is important to me and the effect it has on my life. Please be assured that this is my own personal view, and I am not trying to impose my lifestyle on any one of you – I simply want to make you aware of some things that you may not have considered before.

I'm nothing special: 26 years old, a history teacher and a keen amateur athlete with 800m as my main event. Here is my story of my relationship with food and why, five years ago, I decided to follow a vegan diet. Before going any further, I should explain briefly what this involves. Veganism means following a strict dietary approach which completely eliminates all animal products, including meat, dairy, eggs and honey; it is based on strong ethical principles.

So, how did I end up following this way of life? As a child and teenager, I didn't give much thought to diet, nutrition or cooking in general. I ate the same as most of my friends – fatty foods, ready-made meals such as shop-bought pizzas, burgers from fast-food outlets and so on. I did not study Home Economics as an option at school nor did I learn anything about nutrition – a subject I now think should be compulsory in any school curriculum. It's safe to say that my lifestyle was not a healthy one.

It was only after leaving university and starting to work full-time that I became aware of the importance of nutrition in our lives and how a healthy and balanced diet could have a positive influence on not just my physical health but also on my mental outlook. I talked to colleagues – especially those in the Biology and Home Economics departments – and read all I could find on nutrition and diet. I learned about different types of nutrients, and the importance of eating carefully balanced meals throughout the day. I began to understand how what we eat to give us our daily energy greatly affects our overall physical and mental health. I soon decided to eliminate meat from my meals and began to follow a vegetarian diet.

I quickly became aware of feeling healthier, and continued my research into nutrition. A couple of years ago, the benefits of adopting a fully vegan diet became apparent to me. One thing that attracted me, in particular, was that scientific research emphasised that such a diet could improve not just my overall health but also my performance as an athlete. Once I adopted a vegan diet, I soon became aware of a difference – my recovery time from a race greatly improved; I suffered less from muscle soreness and, most satisfyingly, I was able to increase my training schedule without any ill effects. As a result, my overall athletic performance has improved significantly, I have more energy and I'm feeling much healthier.

I now also understand how people following a vegan diet can help improve the health of our planet about which I care deeply. Following such a diet contributes not only to the reduction of our carbon footprint but also benefits land use and water use. I am now fully committed to following a diet completely free of all animal and fish products – a belief reinforced by what I have also learnt about the cruelty animals suffer as a result of some farming methods.

Directed writing exercises

1 Your cousin who lives in another town is trying to decide whether or not to take up a vegan diet and has asked for your advice. This is a purely personal decision and there are no religious reasons influencing your cousin's decision. However, you know that your cousin is very concerned about the environment, the future of the planet and the ways human beings can cause damage to it.

You have no strong views either way about the subject of veganism. Write an email to your cousin in which you give reasons for and against changing to a vegan diet. In your email you should include:

- reasons for changing to a vegan diet

- reasons for continuing to eat meat

- what you think would be the most suitable choice for your cousin and your reasons for making this suggestion.

Continue writing on a separate sheet of paper if necessary.

3 Writing summaries

Student book, Units 3, 6 and 8

Writing a summary

The purpose of writing a summary is to show evidence that you:

- have understood what you have read
- can select the relevant information
- can express the information using your own words and in a shorter form than the original passage.

The guidance that follows is a review of the advice about writing summaries given in the student book. The points are given here to remind you of how you should approach summary writing tasks.

Step 1: Read the question carefully

This is very important, as it is unlikely that you will be required to summarise the whole of the original passage. The wording of the question will direct you towards the points you should include. For example, the whole passage may be about everyday life in Japan, but you may be asked to summarise only what it tells you about going to school in that country. You must, therefore, keep the wording of the question clearly in mind when reading the passage.

Step 2: Read right through the passage(s) once

This will allow you to gain a good overall understanding of what the material is about.

Step 3: Identify the information that is relevant

Refresh your memory of what the question asks you to do and then read through the passage again very carefully. At this stage you should underline or highlight on the question paper all the information that is relevant to the question. You must be ruthless. Ignore anything that is not relevant, no matter how interesting you may find it. It may help if you give your summary a title.

Step 4: Make notes in your own words

Now is the time to put pen to paper. You should make rough notes of the points you have identified, using your own words as far as possible.

Remember, the use of your own words is important as this is a way of showing that you have understood the passage(s). Try to:

- paraphrase (rephrase) parts of the text to which you refer
- use synonyms – words with the same meaning – instead of the exact words from the text.

This will make it very clear that you understand what you have read.

You do not have to use your own words when making notes but you may find that it will help when writing your final summary if you do so. You should make the notes in the space for planning your answer in the exam answer booklet but your plan will not be marked by an examiner.

Step 5: Count the main points

Once you have noted all the main points, count how many you have identified.

If you have identified 12 points and you are aiming to write a summary of about 120 words, then, as a rough guide, try to write about ten words for each point.

Step 6: Write the summary

Once you have written rough notes in your own words, you should write them up as a piece of continuous prose, trying to keep your expression as concise as possible. If your notes are sufficiently detailed, this may only be a fine-tuning job.

Step 7: Final check

Once you have written your summary, read it through to check that it makes sense. You may not have to count the number of words you wrote. If, for example, you know that you usually write about eight words per line, then a quick count up of the number of lines you have filled will give some indication of how many words you have written in total.

> **Key point**
>
> It is important that you try to keep within the suggested word limit. A very long answer will almost certainly contain irrelevant material and repetition. An answer that has significantly fewer than the suggested number of words will have left out key points.

Marks available

Summary writing is tested in the first part of Question 2, Paper 1 of the Cambridge IGCSE First Language English examination. You will need to demonstrate your understanding of what you have read in Text B of the insert and you will also gain marks for your written expression. There are 10 marks available for reading and 5 marks for written expression. The reading marks are not necessarily awarded on a mark per point basis but will take into account the range of points you have made and how effectively they have been selected to give an overview of the main ideas of the passage that are relevant to the subject of the summary. The marks for writing will be awarded for the focus and organisation of your response and also for how clearly and accurately you have expressed your points.

The second half of Question 2 is not part of the summary exercise but tests your understanding of some of the vocabulary used in the passage. This is worth a further 5 marks.

The passage for summary (Text B) will be about 350–400 words in length and your summary should not exceed 120 words.

Summary writing exercises

Please note – in all the following exercises, Question 1 encourages you to make appropriate notes on the passage as the basis for your summary as this is best practice. Question 2 requires you to write the summary itself and it is only on this question that marks will be awarded.

Exercise 1

Read the following extract carefully and then answer the questions that follow.

Langkawi Island

Langkawi Island is part of an archipelago situated off the north-west coast of Malaysia. I was fortunate enough to spend some time there on a work project and although this meant spending much of the day in meeting rooms, there was also free time when we were able to appreciate the beauty of a place that epitomised my idea of what a tropical island has to offer its visitors.

Langkawi is now one of the most important of Malaysia's holiday destinations and attracts tourists from around the world offering wide, clean sandy beaches, a range of hotels and beach resorts and excellent diving opportunities. It was only comparatively recently, however, that the island became known to the wider world.

Despite being the largest of the 99 islands that make up the archipelago, it never developed into a great trading centre such as Penang and Malacca. In earlier times it attracted traders bringing spices and silks from China and India but the trade declined, perhaps because of fear

3 WRITING SUMMARIES

→ of the pirates who hid in its concealed coves, or maybe there were other reasons for Langkawi being avoided by travellers and merchants.

Like most visitors, we arrived by direct flight from Kuala Lumpur, which took about an hour. We were taken to our hotel by taxi, and on our drive around the edge of an azure blue lagoon we passed palm trees and rice paddy fields where water buffalo lay resting surrounded by pure white egrets. In the distance we could see wooden houses built on stilts over the water.

Although our work commitments prevented us from spending much time idling away on the long stretches of white sand beaches, Langkawi is a compact place and we, nevertheless, found opportunity to experience many of its charms. Families of monkeys of all ages abound, including long-tailed macaques, especially in the rain forest which was within easy reach of our hotel. We soon learnt not to leave our bags unattended when we were sitting in the outside area as they are curious, to say the least!

One free afternoon we took a boat trip to one of the nearby islands and travelled through a dense mangrove forest past Flying Fox Island where we could see innumerable huge bats (the 'flying foxes'), many of them hanging from the trees – their wing spans can grow to 1.2 metres. In the distance, we also saw small 'mangrove dogs' (Malay dingos), rust-brown in colour and light enough to run across the swamp without sinking. We also heard that the mangrove forests were inhabited by other wildlife such as pythons, monitor lizards and crocodiles, although we did not see any of these. At all times on the trip, we were accompanied by gangs of monkeys.

Langkawi is also an island of legends, the most prominent of which is the story of Mahsuri, whose mausoleum, Makam Mahsuri, can be found on the island. She was a beautiful young girl who came from Thailand (Siam) in the 1800s to be married to the son of a tribal chief. She was loved by all who met her apart from her mother-in-law who was jealous of her beauty and innocence, and accused her of being unfaithful to her husband. As a result of these lies, the innocent Mahsuri was sentenced to death and at her execution laid a curse on the island that it would not prosper for seven generations – this curse is perhaps another reason, apart from pirates, why Langkawi remained unknown for so long. Langkawi's fortunes did, in fact, only start to improve in the 1990s, after the film 'Anna and the King' starring Jodie Foster was filmed there. In the mausoleum can be seen clippings from contemporary English newspapers verifying the wrongful execution of Mahsuri along with evidence of her family history.

Another legend concerns the Lake of the Pregnant Maiden, the bright green, fresh waters of which can be seen in the depths of the forest. It is said that an ethereal princess, Mambang Sari, married a mortal prince. The couple were blessed with a baby boy who tragically died soon after birth. The princess buried the baby in the lake and before returning to her home in the skies blessed the waters of the lake so that any young maiden who wishes for a child will have her wish granted if she bathes there.

One more amusing legend concerns Kuah, the island's main town. The Malay meaning of the town's name is 'gravy' and derives from the story of two giants who upset a pot of gravy in this place. The two highest mountains of the island are named after these two giants. Also in the town can be found Taman Lagenda (Legends Park) which contains exhibits of the myths of the island.

We had a successful and satisfying week working in Langkawi but our time there was greatly enhanced by what we learnt of the culture of the island and the scenery and wildlife that contributed so much to our experience there.

Summary writing exercises

1 Notes and planning

What do you learn about the legends of Langkawi and the wildlife that can be found there from the passage? Use the space below to plan your answer.

2 Now write a summary of what the passage tells you about the legends of Langkawi and the wildlife that can be found there.

You should write no more than 250 words. Continue writing on a separate sheet of paper if necessary.

3 WRITING SUMMARIES

Exercise 2
Read the following passage carefully and then answer the questions that follow.

The Peanut Man

George Washington Carver was born into slavery in Missouri around 1864. A sickly child, who often fell ill, Carver was unable to work in the fields, so he did household chores and gardening instead. He was left with many free hours to wander the woods – beginning a lifelong love affair with nature. He had a secret garden where he grew all kinds of things. People would ask him for advice about growing healthy plants. After slavery was abolished in Missouri in 1865, Carver left the state at the age of 12 to pursue an education. In 1890, he began to study music and art at Simpson College in Iowa.

Painting enabled him to combine his two loves – art and nature – but it was his interest in growing things that led him in 1891 to become the first African-American to enrol on a farming methods course at Iowa State University. He was an excellent student and soon started his academic career as the university's first African-American lecturer.

Later, he taught at Tuskegee Institute in Alabama and put his plant skills to good use. There were many cotton plantations in the southern states of the USA. As cotton plants use up most of the nutrients in the soil, it becomes 'worn out' after a few years. Eventually, cotton will no longer grow in this soil. African-American farmers who supported themselves and their families by selling cotton were therefore facing difficulties. Carver decided to help them and came up with a plan. He knew that certain plants, such as peanuts, put nutrients back into the soil. Peanuts are also an excellent source of protein. Carver realised that planting peanuts would help to restore the soil, provide food for farm animals, and protein for the farmers and their families.

For much of the 19th century, peanuts were not grown as a farm crop in the United States, but Carver changed that. He told farmers to rotate their crops by planting cotton one year, then peanuts and other soil-restoring plants, like peas and sweet potatoes the following year. This idea worked. Peanuts grew very well and added enough nutrients to the soil for cotton to grow the following year. Carver also had a plan as to how farmers could find a market for their surplus stocks of peanuts.

Through his knowledge of science, and by separating the fats, oils and sugars in the nuts, he went on to propose more than 300 uses for the humble peanut. He thought up recipes using peanuts including peanut sausage and coffee. He suggested making cosmetics such as face powder from them, and thought glue and axle grease could also be made from peanuts.

Although only a small number of these suggested peanut products were ever put into production, he certainly helped spread the word about peanuts. Carver suggested making peanut paste, but did not, however, invent peanut butter.

By 1920, the many peanut farmers in the USA formed the United Peanut Association of America. In 1921 Carver addressed the US Congress about the many uses for peanuts and the Peanut Man, as he was known, became famous throughout the nation. By 1940 peanuts were one of the top six crops in the USA.

In the last years of his life, Carver became a minor celebrity. In 1941, his achievements were mentioned in *Time* magazine. He was a close friend of Henry Ford, a fellow inventor. He was the first non-president to have a monument established at his birthplace by the National Park Service. Two decades after his death, the opera singer Marian Anderson christened a nuclear submarine that bore his name.

His focus, however, was always on helping people. He travelled the South to promote racial harmony, and to India to discuss nutrition in developing nations with Mahatma Gandhi. When he died on 5 January 1943, Carver's research had won him worldwide acclaim. He is buried on the university campus at Tuskegee where he donated his life savings to establish a research institute.

3 WRITING SUMMARIES

1 Notes and planning

What do you learn about the life, achievements and reputation of George Washington Carver? Use the space below to plan your answer.

2 Now write a summary of what the passage tells you about the life, achievements and reputation of George Washington Carver.

You should write no more than 250 words. Continue writing on a separate sheet of paper if necessary.

....

....

....

....

....

....

....

....

3 WRITING SUMMARIES

Exercise 3
Read the following extract carefully and then answer the questions that follow.

Mysteries of the sea

In April 2007, the 12-metre yacht, *Kaz II*, was found drifting 130 kilometres off the east Australian coastline, with no sign of its crew of three.

On board, the engine was running, the table was set for a meal and a computer was open and running. Apart from a torn sail, there were no signs of anything wrong on the boat. The crew have never been found, and no explanation has ever been given for their disappearance.

The yacht had set off three days before to sail around Northern Australia to Western Australia. Many theories have been advanced. The fact that fenders were down led to suggestions that *Kaz II* had been boarded by another boat and her crew were victims of foul play. Clothes were found neatly folded on the deck. Another theory was that the three crew known to be on board had all taken a swim together. Other theories were that the yacht became stuck on a sandbank, and the men jumped overboard to push her free, but a gust of wind blew the vessel away from them, or that one fell overboard and the others were lost trying to save him. Instruments on board showed that the yacht had not been steered since the day of her departure; she had, therefore, been drifting for three full days before she was found. The mystery has never been solved.

Another mystery was that of the *Marie Celeste*, a large sailing vessel, discovered in the Atlantic Ocean in 1872, unmanned and under full sail, drifting towards Gibraltar. Of her people on board nothing has ever been learned. She had sailed with a captain and a crew of seven, plus the captain's wife and two-year-old daughter.

The ship had set off on 5 November from New York, heading for Genoa. Just a month later, she was discovered drifting by another sailing ship, the *Dei Gratia*. The crew boarded the ship, finding her in generally good condition. One lifeboat had been launched, and the captain's instruments were missing. The *Marie Celeste* was world news at the time, but no conclusions were ever reached. Some suspicion fell on the crew of the *Dei Gratia* and they were rewarded only one fifth of what they should have received for bringing the ship home.

Adapted from www.sail-world.com/UK

Summary writing exercises

1 Notes and planning

What do you learn about the *Kaz II* and the *Marie Celeste* and about what people think may have happened to them from the passage? Use the space below to plan your answer.

2 Now write a summary of what the passage tells you about the *Kaz II* and the *Marie Celeste* and about what people think may have happened to them.

You should write no more than 150 words. Continue writing on a separate sheet of paper if necessary.

3 WRITING SUMMARIES

Exercise 4

Read the following passage carefully and then answer the questions that follow.

Why people in 'blue zones' live longer than people in the rest of the world

'Blue Zone' is a non-scientific term given to regions of the world where some of the world's oldest people live, where there are lower rates of chronic diseases and a longer life expectancy. The term was first used by the author Dan Buettner, who was studying areas of the world in which people live exceptionally long lives; they are called Blue Zones because during their research Buettner and his colleagues drew blue circles around them on a map.

Overall, five main Blue Zone areas have been identified: the Greek island of Icaria whose people eat a diet rich in olive oil and homegrown vegetables. Another island Blue Zone is in the mountainous Ogliastra region of Sardinia where some of the oldest men in the world live. Their work is mainly outdoors as they are farmers.

Some of the world's oldest women can be found in Okinawa in Japan; they practise tai chi (a meditative exercise) and their diet is mainly soy-based foods. Other areas where it would seem diet plays a part in longevity are the Nicoya Peninsula in Costa Rica where beans and corn tortillas are a staple of people's diet and Loma Linda in California where there is a tight-knit religious community of Seventh-day Adventists who are strict vegetarians. Other factors that possibly contribute to the long lives of people in these areas are that they do physical outdoor work and have different types of meditative, spiritual lifestyles.

It appears, therefore, that environmental influences, including diet and lifestyle, play a huge role in determining your lifespan. One thing common to people living in Blue Zones is that those who live there although not necessarily vegetarians, primarily eat a 95 per cent plant-based diet. A number of research studies have shown that avoiding red meat and processed meat can significantly reduce the risk of death from a number of serious illnesses.

Having a diet based on the following food types as eaten by people living in Blue Zones, however, would appear to influence significantly the chances of living a long life: vegetables and legumes (beans, peas, lentils and chick peas) are full of fibre and many different vitamins and minerals; whole grains are also rich in fibre and can reduce blood pressure and heart disease; nuts are important sources of fibre and contribute to a balanced diet.

Other aspects of the diets and lifestyles of Blue Zone people are that they eat fish which contains omega-3 fats and is good for brain and heart health. They also frequently have a reduced calorie intake and some will stop eating when they feel 80 per cent full, which prevents them from eating too many calories, which can result in weight gain and chronic disease. It has also been observed that the habit of eating slowly can reduce hunger and increase feelings of fullness. In a similar way, Blue Zone people tend to eat their smallest meal late in the day and then eat no more until the following day.

Exercise is another important factor in ageing. People in the Blue Zones have exercise built into their daily lives through activities such as gardening and walking in the hilly districts where many of them live rather than by visiting a gym.

A good night's sleep is also considered important for a long and healthy life. In addition to exercise, getting adequate rest and a good night's sleep also seem to be very important for living a long and healthy life. People living in the Blue Zones take naps as and when their body tells them to, rather than living a regular lifestyle with set hours for sleep and work. It appears to be important, however, that their daytime naps do not exceed 30 minutes – if they are much longer they may have negative effects on the heart.

3 WRITING SUMMARIES

> → Finally, a number of other life-enhancing factors are common to the Blue Zones. These include having a strong and shared life-purpose (which may improve their mental health); living in family groups where grandparents look after their grandchildren; having a healthy social network – for example, if your friends keep fit, it is likely that you will do so as well.
>
> The Blue Zone regions are home to some of the oldest and healthiest people in the world. By adopting some of the factors mentioned above into your lifestyle, you may add a few years to your own life.

1 Notes and planning

What have you learned about Blue Zones, the lifestyle habits of people who live in them and the health benefits they provide? Use the space below to plan your answer.

2 Now write a summary of what the passage tells you about Blue Zones, the lifestyle habits of people who live in them and the health benefits they provide.

You should write no more than 250 words. Continue writing on a separate sheet of paper if necessary.

3 WRITING SUMMARIES

Exercise 5
Read the following passage carefully and then answer the questions that follow.

Sea turtles – an endangered species

Sea turtles have inhabited our oceans for more than 110 million years; they are reptiles belonging to the order, *Testudines*. There are, at present, seven species in existence: the flatback, green, hawksbill, leatherback, loggerhead, Kemp's ridley and olive ridley turtles. The leatherback is the largest in size and the Kemp's ridley is the smallest. All species of turtles, with the exception of the flatback, are listed as endangered and/or threatened under the Endangered Species Act with the most endangered being the Kemp's ridley sea turtle, the hawksbill turtle, and the green sea turtle. Worldwide, about 61 per cent of all turtles, both land and sea dwelling, are in danger of becoming extinct. For example, about two centuries ago, the Caribbean Sea was inhabited by tens of millions of sea turtles and now its population has been reduced to merely tens of thousands. A similar decline has been noticed in other seas which provide a home for the creatures.

What have turtles done to incur such a threat to the very existence of their species? The answer is, nothing – other than being unable to adapt to the changes to the world in which they live. Although only a handful of countries around the world allow turtle fishing as a legal activity, it nevertheless results in about 40 000 turtles a year being caught for human consumption. Considerably more, however, are poached illegally, both for their meat and eggs but also for their shells, which can be turned into fashion items, all of which are sources of food and income for the poachers.

But there are also other less obvious causes for turtles' decline in numbers resulting from human activity. Turtles come ashore in certain parts of the world to lay their eggs on sandy beaches so that their young are able to breathe oxygen. However, as a species, they are particularly susceptible to light pollution, which is increasing in the areas they have traditionally chosen for nesting. These areas are also subject to development and pollution which degrade turtle nesting areas with a resultant deleterious effect on their egg-laying.

Although both legal fishing and poaching contribute to the turtles' declining numbers, another related issue is accidental fishing (also known as 'by-catch'). Sea turtles are often caught unintentionally in the nets of fishermen trawling for other fish or shrimps and even caught by those fishing with longline hooks. The fishermen responsible seldom bother to release the turtles they have caught and simply leave them to die. Even if the fishers try to release the accidentally caught turtles it is often too late to save their lives, as they will have been deprived for too long of the oxygen they need. According to a 2020 report by the Worldwide Fund for Nature (WWF) and Sky Ocean Rescue, over 250 000 turtles die each year as a result of by-catch.

A further threat to turtles is the unsustainable development of coastal areas for hotels and high-rise apartment blocks, which involve an increase in boat traffic, dredging, etc. and also the presence of building vehicles which compact the sand on the beaches. All these factors can seriously damage the turtles' traditional nesting habitats.

Pollution from plastic waste dumped in the oceans can cause serious harm to the turtles' specialised diets. Turtles ingest plastic bags mistaking them for jellyfish or sponges as well as consuming smaller plastic waste thinking it to be fish or algae. It has been estimated that up to 52 per cent of sea turtles have ingested plastic waste.

Coastal building projects cause additional problems. The increase in artificial light pollution increases the threat to nesting sea turtles as light from buildings disturbs and prevents the females from nesting, and if they do, the light can cause the baby turtles to be confused and to lose their sense of direction so that they wander away from the sea.

Summary writing exercises

> Although the Endangered Species Act has done much to help preserve turtle species, there is still a long way to go. As organisations such as the WWF fully understand, it is vitally important to raise peoples' awareness of the plight of turtles and to work alongside local communities to develop local money-making opportunities that do not rely on turtle harvesting.
>
> We can also play our part by learning about more eco-friendly seafood choices from the Marine Stewardship Council, and encouraging our friends and their families to be aware of the importance of sustainable fishing and eco-friendly seafood choices. We can support turtle-friendly tourism to places that make provision for protecting turtle nests and which turn lights off at night, closely monitor turtles in the area and advise guests on how to behave around them. We should limit our use of plastics, especially plastic bags, and take part in regular beach clean-ups.

1 Notes and planning

What have you learned about sea turtles, the reasons that that they are an endangered species and what people can do to help them survive? Use the space below to plan your answer.

2 Now write a summary of what the passage tells you about sea turtles, the reasons that that they are an endangered species and what people can do to help them survive.

You should write no more than 250 words. Continue writing on a separate sheet of paper if necessary.

3 WRITING SUMMARIES

Exercise 6

Read the following passage carefully and then answer the questions that follow.

Timbuktu – then and now

'Timbuktu' – just the name of this distant city, sited on the southern edge of the Sahara Desert 20 kilometres north of the Niger River, conjures up images of a mythical, faraway paradise, of gold, learning and romantic adventure, in the minds of many people.

The city is now part of the country of Mali and has been in existence for over a thousand years, being first established in the early 12th century when it developed from a nomadic trading centre. It is a place of sand-coloured towers and dusty streets which make it appear to have grown out of the very desert that surrounds it. Over the centuries it grew from a seasonal encampment for nomadic merchants into a major centre for caravan trade and a place of culture and learning. Its reputation grew and reached its peak in the 14th and 15th centuries as merchants and scholars from throughout the continent of Europe were attracted there.

Salt from mines in the east was one of the main commodities traded in Timbuktu, for gold brought in by merchants and travellers from Europe. At the time, the city was prospering and seemed to contain endless wealth and resources. A 14th century visitor describes Timbuktu as a busy, bustling trading centre. In the minds of Europeans living during a time of bubonic plague and unusually cold weather, it was a mythical, romantic place with its streets paved with gold.

The 'Golden Age' of Timbuktu reached its peak in the second half of the 15th century and it was the result not only of the city's economic wealth but also of its culture and learning. There were nearly 200 *maktabs* (Quranic schools) in the city at which hundreds of international scholars came to study; they worked as scribes and produced a great number of manuscripts that resulted in a vast library. Visitors to the city were treated as honoured guests and exchanged their learning and their books with the resident scholars, resulting in Timbuktu becoming one of the world's great centres of learning.

In 1591, however, the city was invaded and subjugated by Moroccan troops and subsequently its fortunes went into a long decline which continued into the 20th century. Although Western travellers and explorers, still drawn by romantic myths of the legendary city, continued to make the challenging journey there across the desert sand, they discovered on arrival that it was far less grand than they had imagined. Tropical diseases such as malaria flourished in the area and the trading boom was in terminal decline. Frequent droughts had reduced the city's water supplies and this contributed to the health problems of those who both lived and visited there. One traveller recorded, 'Everything exuded the greatest sadness. I was surprised by the lack of activity, the inertia that reigned in the city.'

In the latter half of the 20th century, the city was afflicted by even more severe droughts and when it seemed that things had reached their lowest point, in 2012 extremists invaded and caused great damage to the city's cultural heritage by burning thousands of ancient manuscripts and other artefacts.

Nevertheless, Timbuktu has managed to survive and there are some signs of recovery. In recent years, inhabitants who fled the rule of the extremists have now returned to their homes. Because of the damage caused earlier in the century and the poverty which affects many who live there, many travellers are still unwilling to travel to Timbuktu as some Western embassies have advised

3 WRITING SUMMARIES

> their citizens against doing so. However, there remains hope for the city's recovery. An American, Alexandra Huddleston, who visited in 2007, suggested that the city's centuries of tradition may still help it to revive and survive. Although it may never regain the intellectual and economic glories of previous centuries, there remains hope that 'the mythic image of Timbuktu seems likely to endure indefinitely: legendary crossroad of the Sahara, city of gold and knowledge.'

1 Notes and planning

What have you learned about the importance of Timbuktu, the history of the city and why it attracted so many visitors throughout the ages? Use the space below to plan your answer.

2 Now write a summary of what the passage tells you about the importance of Timbuktu, and history of the city and why it attracted so many visitors throughout the ages.

You should write no more than 250 words. Continue writing on a separate sheet of paper if necessary.

....

....

....

....

....

....

4 Writing compositions

Student book, Units 4, 9, 11 and 12

The directed writing tasks that you practised earlier allow you both to show your understanding of what someone else has written and to demonstrate your own skills as a writer, in particular through argumentative or persuasive writing. Another key writing skill that you should develop is to write something original based on your own imagination or experience in a descriptive or narrative essay which will be judged only for how effectively you have expressed yourself in writing. When presenting your work, it is important that you cover both content and structure, and style and accuracy.

As a general rule, you should write 350–450 words and it is a good idea to keep your response within this limit when you are writing under timed conditions. Writing too much will almost certainly lead to a response that is lacking in organisation and contains avoidable errors of expression.

To remind you, here are the assessment objectives for writing:

W1 Articulate experience and express what is thought, felt and imagined.

W2 Organise and structure facts, ideas and opinions for deliberate effect.

W3 Use a range of vocabulary and sentence structures appropriate to context.

W4 Use language appropriate to purpose and to engage the audience.

W5 Make accurate use of spelling, punctuation and grammar.

> **Key point**
>
> You must choose to write either a narrative or a descriptive piece of writing. When writing an imaginative essay, it is important not to confuse the features of descriptive and narrative writing. In particular, you should avoid including excessive narrative detail when attempting a descriptive task. It is acceptable to use a general narrative structure (for example, a first-person description of different aspects of a scene as you, the writer, move from place to place), but the main focus should be descriptive.
>
> You should only write a story in response to a narrative topic. If you attempt a narrative topic, it is vitally important that you plan events carefully before you start to write, and that you keep the time constraints and recommended word limit clearly in mind. Do not try to write a story that is too complicated for the time available.

Structure

An important skill when you are writing compositions is to focus on organising what you write into a coherent sequence so that a reader can clearly follow your train of thought. Remember: whatever you write and for whatever purpose, it is important to keep your readers in mind – they will not be able to fully understand your ideas if your writing is muddled and unplanned. Organising your ideas into logically structured paragraphs that are linked into a coherent whole is of the utmost importance.

The following two exercises will help you to think about structuring a piece of writing.

Exercise 1

The following steps are taken from a recipe describing how to make pancakes, but they are not presented in a logical sequence.

1 Read through the steps and then reorganise them into the correct order.

The correct order is: ....

2 Rewrite the steps as two paragraphs of continuous prose as part of an email to your younger brother, describing how he should cook pancakes for his friends. (You might like to try the recipe yourself as a reward for all your hard work answering the questions in this workbook!)

1	Crack 2 or 3 eggs into a bowl, beat until fluffy. Add the 500 grams of self-raising flour. Do not stir mixture at this point.	6	Enjoy! Try adding butter, peanut butter, syrup, jam, chocolate chips, cookie or candy crumbles or fruit to your pancakes for a different, more exciting flavour. The varieties are endless. These are the most delectable pancakes you will ever taste.
2	Sprinkle a few drops of water onto your pan. If it 'dances', or jumps from the pan with a sizzle, the pan is ready for the batter.	7	Add the butter and 350 ml of milk to the mix. Stir gently, leaving some small clumps of dry ingredients in the batter. Do not blend until completely smooth. If your batter is smooth, your pancakes will be tough and flat as opposed to fluffy.
3	Cook the other side until golden and then remove. If you want a deeper colour, cook for another 30 seconds per side until the pancake is done enough for your taste.	8	Melt 2 tablespoons of butter in a microwave-safe bowl. Make sure that it is completely melted; about 1 minute is sufficient.
4	Heat a frying pan to a medium heat. Be sure to use non-stick spray, or a pat of butter, so the pancakes won't stick.	9	Pour about 4 tablespoons of batter from the tip of a large spoon, or from a jug, onto a hot griddle or greased frying pan. The amount you pour will decide the final size of your pancake. It is best to begin with less batter, and then slowly pour more batter into the pan to increase the pancake size.
5	Cook for about 2 minutes or until the pancake is golden. You should see bubbles form and then pop around the edges. When the bubbles at the edge of the batter pop and a hole is left that does not immediately close up, flip the pancake gently.		

4 WRITING COMPOSITIONS

....

....

....

....

....

....

....

....

....

....

....

....

....

....

....

....

....

Exercise 2

Opposite are seven paragraphs taken from an account of the history of the town of Port Royal in Jamaica as a home for pirates. The paragraphs, however, are out of their original sequence. Read them carefully and then reorganise them. The first and last paragraphs are in the right place; you should rearrange the other five in a logical order.

A logical order is: ....

Vocabulary

1	If you go to Jamaica for a vacation you must investigate what is left of the infamous 'lost pirate city' of Port Royal. It was one of the largest coastal towns in the Caribbean in the 17th and 18th centuries.	5	As the population grew, it became a very wealthy town owing to its sea trade. By the mid-1600s it was said to have over 5000 residents. Sources say there were over 2000 buildings crowded together, some made of brick and up to four storeys tall. Port Royal also soon owned a wicked reputation for the pirates and privateers who frequented its harbour.
2	For a number of years privateering was a legitimate business; captains of privately owned warships were granted official approval allowing them to attack ships flying enemy flags. Their cargos and the vessels themselves could be seized and sold for a considerable profit. Eventually, in 1684, France, Spain and England signed a treaty which agreed to an end to hostilities in the West Indies. Legal piracy was no more. However, as many captains and crews did not wish to so easily give up their ventures, piracy continued on the blue waters of the Caribbean.	6	From Port Royal, Jamaica the 'Brotherhood of the Coast' (as pirates were called in those days) sailed out and raided wealthy merchant vessels and the famous Spanish war ships crossing the seas between Europe and the 'New World'.
3	When they returned to their sanctuary, no mortal dared enter Port Royal in pursuit, as it was guarded by four forts. This pirate haven was one of the best defended ports in the world and most feared.	7	One of the most famous pirates to have his base at Port Royal was Sir Henry Morgan. Many called him 'the Pirate King', as he amassed a great fortune as well as respect from his many sea battles and raiding ventures. However, once he was knighted by the English King, Charles II, he tried to make the region more respectable by attempting to remove the criminals. He began to hunt down his old pirate buddies and hanged them at Gallows Point. It would be at Morgan's hands that the streets of Port Royal and the story of the pirates would forever change. Eventually he was made Governor of Jamaica.
4	In the Golden Days of Pirates it was called 'the richest and wickedest city in the world'. Men of all races and cultures came to this port to trade their treasures and booty, most looted on the high seas from Spanish and British ships.		

Adapted from 'The Lost Pirate City of Port Royal Jamaica'

Vocabulary

One of the most important points to remember when you write is to try to express your meaning as precisely as possible. This requires thinking carefully about the vocabulary that you use, and how your intended meaning can be affected by your choice of words and the associations that different words can have in the minds of your readers.

Exercise 3

The following passage is taken from the opening chapter of Charles Dickens's novel *Bleak House*. It is a description of 19th-century London, which the writer wants to present to his readers as a thoroughly unpleasant city full of fog and mud.

You will notice that certain words that help to convey this impression have been omitted from the passage. As you read through the description, think of your own words to fill the gaps. Once you have done this, compare your version with Dickens's (included in the Workbook Answers, which your teacher will have access to) and then try to decide which vocabulary choices are more effective and why. (Note: this exercise will also help in preparing you for answering questions about a writer's use of language.)

4 WRITING COMPOSITIONS

As much mud in the streets as if the waters had but newly retired from the face of the earth, and it would not be wonderful to meet a Megalosaurus, forty feet long or so, ... like an elephantine lizard up Holborn Hill. Smoke, ... down from chimney-pots, making a soft black drizzle, with flakes of soot in it as big as full-grown snowflakes – gone into mourning, one might imagine, for the death of the sun. Dogs, ... in mire. Horses, scarcely better; splashed to their very blinkers. Foot passengers, ... one another's umbrellas in a general infection of ill temper, and losing their foot-hold at street-corners, where tens of thousands of other foot passengers have been slipping and sliding since the day broke (if the day ever broke), adding new deposits to the .... of mud, sticking at those points, ... to the pavement, and accumulating at compound interest.

Fog everywhere. Fog up the river, where it flows among green aits [small islands] and meadows; fog down the river, where it .... defiled among the tiers of shipping and the waterside pollutions of a great (and dirty) city. Fog on the Essex marshes, fog on the Kentish heights. Fog .... into the cabooses [ships' kitchens] of collier-brigs; fog lying out on the yards and hovering in the rigging of great ships; fog .... on the gunwales of barges and small boats. Fog in the eyes and throats of ancient Greenwich pensioners, ... by the firesides of their wards; fog in the stem and bowl of the afternoon pipe of the wrathful skipper, down in his close cabin; fog .... pinching the toes and fingers of his shivering little 'prentice boy on deck. Chance people on the bridges .... over the parapets into a nether sky of fog, with fog all round them, as if they were up in a balloon and hanging in the misty clouds.

Gas .... through the fog in divers places in the streets, much as the sun may, from the .... fields, be seen to loom by husbandman and ploughboy. Most of the shops lighted two hours before their time – as the gas seems to know, for it has a .... and .... look.

From *Bleak House* by Charles Dickens

Accuracy of expression

Accuracy in spelling, punctuation and grammar in all your writing is important as errors of this sort can easily result in a reader becoming confused and your intended meaning being lost. As part of your preparation, it is important that you think carefully about the types of errors that you are prone to make in your expression. Do your best to avoid a careless approach that can cause you to make errors, especially when you are writing hurriedly and under pressure.

Exercise 4

Here is an extract from a piece of writing by a student. It has been marked by a teacher who has underlined errors of various kinds but has not actually corrected the mistakes. Rewrite the passage, correcting the errors that are indicated. (They are all points that you will have had explained to you in your English lessons during your time at school.)

Lee **returned back** home late that night; he was tired and **laid** down on his bed. It had been a **tireing** day. He had been in the school **since** five years and as a senior student he had been asked to judge the Junior **Pupils** debating competition. Lee was looking forward to his **roll** as a judge. He was determined to remain **uninterested** throughout the competition. '**Its** my opportunity to show how sensible I am and to choose **whose** the best speaker in the Junior School,' he had said to his mother that morning.

The competition had been of a high standard. According to **Lees** notes, none of those taking part scored less than six marks out of ten. It was very hard to decide who was the winner as none of them deserved to **loose** and at least three competitors could **of been** the winners. Lee finally made his decision after much deliberation and gave the name of the winner to the **Principle** of the school, who then presented the prize.

Composition writing exercises

Here is a selection of tasks for you to practise both descriptive and narrative writing. Remember that you should aim to write 350–450 words, so you will need to continue writing your answer on a separate sheet of paper. You should aim to spend no more than 60–80 minutes writing each answer and should also try to write each answer in one continuous session. Do not forget that you should spend some of your time thinking about the task you have chosen and making brief notes of your planned content before you start to write. Try to leave yourself some time to proofread what you have written once you have finished and, in particular, to check for the types of errors that you know you have a tendency to make.

A suggested approach to planning your writing has been provided for the first of the descriptive tasks below, as a guide if you wish to use it.

4 WRITING COMPOSITIONS

Descriptive tasks

1 Describe the inside of your favourite shop and some of the people who work there.

Possible approach to planning:

- It is probably better to choose a small shop rather than a large store. It is easier to focus on a small place rather than trying to select relevant features from a larger one.

- Where is the shop located? What does it sell?

- The task specifically mentions the *inside* of the shop – do not waste time describing the exterior.

- Is it an old or a new building? What are the first impressions as you enter the shop? Is it usually very busy or is it quiet?

- What is the atmosphere like in the shop? Describe the most striking things that you see, the sounds of the shop and any smells that are special to this place.

- Do not try to describe too many of the people who work there. Two will be sufficient. It would be a good idea to choose two who contrast with each other, for example, young/old; male/female. Describe their personalities as well as their appearance. Remember, the person reading your description is highly unlikely to have been to the shop that you describe, so you are free to make up details to make your description as interesting as you can – as long as the made-up details are believable!

- You need a conclusion; for example, you could reflect on why you particularly like this place and why you think it important for it not to change.

Continue writing on a separate sheet of paper if necessary.

2 Describe some members of your neighbour's family and the house in which they live.

Continue writing on a separate sheet of paper if necessary.

4 WRITING COMPOSITIONS

3 Write about your last day at your previous school.

Continue writing on a separate sheet of paper if necessary.

4 Describe a family birthday celebration and some of the people who were present.

Continue writing on a separate sheet of paper if necessary.

4 WRITING COMPOSITIONS

5 Write about a place that makes you feel relaxed and a place that makes you feel uneasy.

Continue writing on a separate sheet of paper if necessary.

Narrative tasks

1 'I knew that I should not have listened to my friend …' Write a story that begins or ends with these words.

Continue writing on a separate sheet of paper if necessary.

4 WRITING COMPOSITIONS

2 'The door at the end of the corridor'. Use this as the title of a narrative.

Continue writing on a separate sheet of paper if necessary.

3 Write a story in which mistaken identity plays a major part.

Continue writing on a separate sheet of paper if necessary.

4 WRITING COMPOSITIONS

4 'The Lost Bag'. Use this as the title of a narrative.

Continue writing on a separate sheet of paper if necessary.

5 'I looked in the mirror and saw ...' Write a story that begins with these words.

Continue writing on a separate sheet of paper if necessary.

Reinforce learning and deepen understanding of the key concepts covered in the latest Cambridge IGCSE™ and IGCSE (9–1) First Language English syllabuses (0500/0990) with this updated Workbook. An ideal course companion or homework book for use throughout the course.

» Develop and strengthen skills and knowledge with a wealth of additional exercises that perfectly supplement the updated Fifth Edition Student's Book.

» Build confidence with extra practice for each lesson to ensure that a topic is thoroughly understood before moving on.

» Consolidate reading comprehension, analysis and evaluation and improve writing skills with practice using a variety of text types and genres.

» Keep track of students' work with ready-to-go write-in exercises.

» Save time with all answers available FREE to download from: www.hachettelearning.com/answers-and-extras.

This text has not been through the endorsement process for the Cambridge Pathway.

Also available:
Cambridge IGCSE First Language English Student's Book, Fifth Edition
9781036010768

The Student's Book is endorsed for the Cambridge Pathway.

For over 30 years we have been trusted by Cambridge schools around the world to provide quality support for teaching and learning.
For this reason we are an Endorsement Partner of Cambridge International Education and publish endorsed materials for their syllabuses.

 Visit us at hachettelearning.com

ISBN 978-1-0360-1078-2